# RESSENTIMENT

# RESSENTIMENT

## MAX SCHELER

*Translation*

Lewis B. Coser
William W. Holdheim

*Introduction*

Manfred S. Frings

*New Edition*

Marquette University Press  —  Milwaukee Wisconsin

Marquette Studies in Philosophy

VII

Andrew Tallon, Series Editor

Printed in the United States of America
ISBN 978-087462-602-5

# TABLE OF CONTENTS

Manfred Frings *Introduction* ............................................................. 1

Prefatory Remarks ..................................................................... 19

I On the Phenomenology and Sociology of *Ressentiment* .......... 23

II *Ressentiment* and Moral Value Judgment.................................... 51

III Christian Morality and *Ressentiment* ....................................... 55

IV *Ressentiment* and Modern Humanitarian Love......................... 79

V *Ressentiment* and Other Value Shifts in Modern Morality......... 97

Notes ...................................................................................... 127

Index...................................................................................... 149

# INTRODUCTION

We are accustomed today to see our tiny planet earth on pictures taken from outer space. During the July 1969 Apollo 11 mission astronaut Edgar Mitchell remarked: "Suddenly from behind the rim of the moon ... there emerges a sparkling blue and white jewel" and what was then a breathtaking photograph showed the earth rising in all its glory — and tragedy.

Many pictures of the kind show us the earth floating through the uncanny tranquillity of the universe; a negligible and quiet star, that is, by comparison to billions of others exploding, imploding, colliding, collapsing, forming. The earth has a distinctive feature. It stands out against its dark background by its shifting blue, white and sometimes reddish colors reflected from the sphere of its air and its water, covering three quarters of its surface.

All scientific and literary visions to the contrary, it might well be the case that it is the only planet in the universe that meets the most subtle and precious conditions for sustaining life. If this could be proven to be the case, say, by a complex mathematical formalism of statistics, no doubt, the human being — which has been the center of twentieth century philosophic inquiry — would have to be assigned a hitherto neglected existential category: the eeriness of cosmic solitude.

So, at least, it looks. But one can take also another step into looking at human existence on the earth. If one removes the earth from such photos, say, by blocking it off from one's mind for a moment, and imagines there just human history alone floating through space, such a vision would solicit the question why, in all the world, humans can be and are so violent, self-destructive, and why they are so foolish to keep on destroying one of their most valuable possessions, their lives and the environment, by waging wars, technology, neglect, or for profit making? The tranquillity of the stars visible above our life-world may be sublime, as Immanuel Kant (1724-1804) held, but human history has no such sublime tranquillity.

The question why there are hate and hostilities among us earthlings, notwithstanding illimitable cultural and scientific achievements, and notwithstanding the counterpoint of human existence: a dormant, or more active, or at least disquieting faith in something Divine, leads one also to ask yet another question: Who are those earthlings when looked at from a bird's eye view, so to speak?

Modern philosophy, taking its historical departure in seventeenth century France with René Descartes (1596-1650), has ever since recognized *reason* to be the essence of being human. This self-understanding of the human race took its root in the cradle of Western civilization: in the philosophy of the ancient Greeks. They taught us that beings endowed with reason are essentially distinguished from the animal kingdom because the latter is devoid of such things as art, culture, history, language, law, religion, or science — all supposedly embedded in human reason.

Up to this day we dwell in this ancient Greek conviction of the power of reason. We firmly believe that we must trust reason alone and everywhere. Without it, there is no progress. Reason allows us to work with explanations of whatever as long as they are logical. Indeed, especially in our own time one takes for granted that everything under the sun is, potentially or in the long run, explainable and controllable by technology as long as reason has accrued enough experience and savvy.

However — and this pertains to the gist of the book before us — rational explanations also hopelessly fail even when they are logically true. Relying on reason alone, as the ancient Greek philosophers suggested, does not exclude its opposite, the non-rational, as is testified by the inexplicability of human tragedy. In contrast to Greek rational philosophy, their literature demonstrates this point over and over again; perhaps, most obviously in the figure of *Antigone*. She represents the unresolvable conflict between laws of reason and feelings. In everyday life pangs of conscience, unexpected deaths, catastrophe, wars, oppressors, massacres, are just some examples of tragedy on our planet.

Yet, Western humanity has a penchant to keep on running after logical, rational explanations. And it must. In contrast to Eastern cultures, it lives more versus than with nature. It prefers to foment passion for knowledge and controlling nature as an object starting with its atoms. It prefers to foment its passion to pry into the human gene. Strangely enough, it does not put the same efforts in exploring the depths of its non-rational sides, exceptions like Freud and others granted.

Max Scheler (1874-1928), by testimony of almost all contemporary European philosophers, was one of the most brilliant thinkers in our century. As Heidegger once put it, there is no present-day philosopher who is not indebted to him. Others agreed with the Spanish philosopher Ortega y Gasset who wrote that with the sudden death of Scheler, Europe had lost one of the greatest minds it ever had. Whereas his name was in circulation everywhere during the twenties, including in Asia and the Americas, his fame faded away like a comet after his demise at the age of fifty-four. He left behind many printed works and thousands of posthumous manuscripts, all of which material was suppressed by the German Nazi regime during 1933 and 1945. Publication of his works took only a slow start in 1954. So did translations of them. As is rather common in the humanities, quickly emerging interests in particular areas and authors who are "in," shifted Scheler's name until recently more into the background of philosophical discussion. To be sure, his studies into the depths of the non-rational, including the tragic of human existence, that is, his investigations into human feelings, emotions, love and hate, did not exactly correlate with twentieth century philosophy characterized by areas like logic, analytic philosophy, the question of being, existentialism, phenomenology, structuralism, deconstruction, etc.

Among Max Scheler's most intriguing early works dealing with the non-rational, emotional depths of human beings is his 1914 investigation into resentment, which increasingly marks the modern era. It was published first in 1912 under the German title, *Ueber Ressentiment und moralisches Werturteil* (Ressentiment and Moral Value-Judgment). In 1915 it went into an enlarged edition with the new title, *Das Ressentiment im Aufbau der Moralen* (The Role of Ressentiment in the Make-Up of Morals). The present Louis A. Coser translation into English is made from the 1915 text. Before the outbreak of World War I (1914-1918), Scheler had also published two other works directly related to our present text: 1) His book *Phenomenology and Theory of Feelings of Sympathy and of Love and Hate*, which received a positive review in *Mind*, California, 1914, and 2) his treatise "Ordo Amoris." Both investigations pry into the darkest spheres of human feelings. Already the titles of these works betray Max Scheler's early preoccupation with human emotions. Contrary to the traditional notion of the rationality of human beingness, he argued that to be human first means to be a "person," and that the traditional definition of the human being as "animal rationale" fails to cover the depths and powers of emotions. After all, every person possesses emotions, emotive reactions, motivations, and uncountable types of feelings of his own. Indeed, deep inside, every person possesses secrets so profound, private, and self-concealing that we never seem to communicate them to others; moreover, persons can conveniently evade admitting them to themselves. Such, indeed, can happen to deeply seated feelings of resentment. In essence, the person is a being of *love*, an "ens amans" for Scheler. In this, he followed in part the French mathematician Blaise Pascal (1623-1662) by drawing a line between "reason," on the one hand, and the seat of all feelings, the "heart," on the other. Western rationalism and intellectualism, argues Scheler, is lopsided. In contrast to Eastern cultures, it lost contact with emotive undercurrents of reason. Hence, Pascal's famous thought that the human heart has its *own* reasons ("le coeur a ses raisons") underlies in large part the present text. But while Pascal just jotted this idea down, Scheler took it up as one of the major points of departure of his investigation into the very complexity of the nature of the human person, that is, the being of the person as spanning reason and heart. His investigations into resentment hold up a mirror against those roots of the human soul from which stalwart rancor is nourished, channeled into feelings that eventually surface in various overt forms of resentment directed against people, social conditions, gender, classes, races, religions, institutions, and even God.

A statement is needed concerning the unique undertone of the French word "ressentiment" as distinguished from English "resentment." The French word possesses a peculiar strong nuance of a lingering hate that our English word "resentment" does not always carry. The German language does not even have a word for "ressentiment." In

German one uses the French word in common speech. French spelling of the word has been preserved in the present translation, and, while reading the text, it is advisable to have the French pronunciation of "ressentiment" in one's ears to preserve the word's peculiar nuance.

Let us cast some light on a few pivots of the background of the text which may lend some additional assistance to its understanding. The pivots belong to Max Scheler's monumental work on value-ethics, published at the same time as the ressentiment-text. The German title translates in English as: *Formalism in Ethics and Non-Formal Ethics of Values. A New Attempt toward the Foundation of an Ethical Personalism* (1913/1916).

## I. THE EMOTIVE STRUCTURE OF RESSENTIMENT IN GENERAL

What, precisely, is ressentiment? The general answer to the question is threefold.

1. Ressentiment is an incurable, persistent feeling of hating and despising which occurs in certain individuals and groups. It takes its root in equally incurable *impotencies* or weaknesses that those subjects constantly suffer from. These impotencies generate either individual or collective, but always negative, emotive attitudes. They can permeate a whole culture, era, and an entire moral system. The feeling of ressentiment leads to false moral judgments made on other people who are devoid of this feeling. Such judgments are not infrequently accompanied by rash, at times fanatical claims of truth generated by the impotency this feeling comes from.

There are various kinds of impotencies from which, strangely enough, the very strength of ressentiment feelings well up. They can be psychic, mental, social, or physical impotencies, disadvantages, weaknesses or deficiencies of various kinds. The individuals and groups concerned suffer from a blockage to communicate with others. They tend to come on slow and, if at all, they can hardly vent what keeps on plaguing them.

2. Any feeling of ressentiment stemming from the impotency in a ressentiment-subject is accompanied by hidden feelings of self-disvalue over against others. The overwhelming dissimilarity between a ressentiment-subject and other people causes a disorder in value experiences and of all feelings conjoined with these disarranged values. In a marked contrast to such a ressentiment-subject, an individual of strong personality has no need to compare himself with his fellow humans, even if they happen to be superior in specific respects and abilities. The strong person is always ready and willing to accept values higher than those he represents. Therefore, no ressentiment can come up. Because of this emotive readiness, he is not easily embarrassed or ashamed about himself. Feelings of resentment, however, are irritated by the *unattainability* of positive values that others represent. Therefore, the inner experiences with others and of himself are in constant disarray. There is always present in ressentiment a disorder of the heart or a "désordre du coeur." That is, ressentiment is a state of constant aberration from the order of values, from the order of feelings and of love, those acts in which the values are first given, i.e., from the "ordo amoris" or the "ordre du coeur." All this amounts to a damaged moral tenor of the individual person constantly charged with ressentiment feelings.

3. The constant state of ressentiment is distinguished sharply from furious reactions or outbursts of anger. Whenever a prosaic resentment-feeling finds satisfaction by way of, say, successful revenge and retaliation, there is no resentment proper at hand. It is therefore not the case that there is ressentiment in those who act out various types of terrorism, as we are so familiar with in our time. Types of terrorism, such as murdering people because of hate, of holding hostages, of placing explosives under parked cars, or the terrorism of devastating whatever may be nearby, etc., happen as a rule because criminals want to find an inner fulfillment in their revengeful terrorism since there are little or no other means to this end. While persons committing acts of violence may entertain a prosaic resentment, one must, reading Scheler's text, come to the conclusion that throughout terrorism resentment is prone to be found among those who do *not* place bombs to kill, etc., but among those who stay behind such acts. Thus, ressenti-

ment-subjects are often to be found among sympathizers of violence rather than among the criminals themselves doing violence.

Let us illustrate the difference between ressentiment and re-sentment by two examples taken from literature.

The short story of one of Scheler's favorite writers, Edgar Allen Poe (1809-1849), "The Cask of Amontillado" may tells us of the re-venge taken by one whose personal honor had been seriously injured. Under the pretense of fun, he later on decides to tie his offender to a wall of a wine cellar, where they had been drinking. Having done so, he then starts to wall him up from the front, slowly and without mercy, and with each brick increasingly enjoys his feelings of revenge. When the last one is laid in place and the offender walled up to die of thirst, suffocation and starvation, the revenge is consumed, and no resentment can well up again. In ressentiment proper, however, no such gratification of revenge occurs. This is because the *impulse* to revenge, but no revenge itself, keeps on simmering without end and relief in sight. The impotency and powerlessness concerned blocks the venom of ressentiment from being washed away by a factual re-venge. Of course, revenge like that in Poe's story can in certain cases be fulfilled over and over again after each revenge taken, and can be suffused with ressentiment. This is the case with certain serial killers whose impulse to take revenge is *not completely* diluted by one kill alone. Resentment is so deep that it can well up again and again after each revenge taken.

Another literary example helps us to come closer to ressentiment. It is Aesop's well known fable of "The Fox and the Grapes," which Scheler alludes to. There are the sweet grapes tempting the fox, but out of his reach. After leaping up and up to get a hold of some, the fox gives up trying. Leaving the scene, he convinces himself that those grapes were not sweet but sour anyway. Aesop's fable comes closer to ressentiment proper, because there is an impotency involved which is at the root of a value-deception. It is a physical impotency, which the fox cannot overcome because he lacks the strength to jump high enough for the grasp of a grape. This makes the fox powerless to taste the grapes' sweetness. The powerlessness, in turn, makes him detract and diminish the value of their sweetness into "sour grapes."

## II. SPECIFIC EMOTIVE STRUCTURES OF RESENTMENT

Within this general description of ressentiment one can discern three specific structures of ressentiment:

1.  A subconscious emotive detraction of a positive value into a negative value.
2.  Ranks among values.
3.  Intersubjective comparing.

Let us look into these specific components.

1. Ressentiment persists and perseveres, it was stated, because of an abiding impotency which blocks any possible realization of particular positive values. This, in turn, lets the venom of ressentiment permeate the person's whole inner life and experience, so that the order of values and the order of loving positive values is in a state of disarray. Reasoning about values cannot stop the emotive disorder from occurring and continuing. It might at best recognize the disorder when, for instance, a ressentiment-subject says, "There is something wrong with me." But this is very rare among those subjects, and it neither nullifies the experience of the disorder felt among positive and negative values, nor does it help to rationally recognize the higher values to be attained, i.e., to let the grapes simply be what they are, namely, sweet. An insight into emotional experiences is a rational inventory of oneself. Rational logic is no cure in a flawed experience of values.

But there is another side to the detraction that lowers unattainable positive values.

While the failure to realize a certain positive value, and while this continues to irk the ressentiment-subject, the feeling of ressentiment also raises those values it indeed can realize; that is, those values that the impotency allows the ressentiment-subject to attain: Giving up trying to reach the unattainable sweetness of the grapes, and the fox's self-deception that they are sour anyway, are more valuable to him than granting the grapes their due. In ordered value-feelings this can also occur because no matter whether the grapes are sweet or sour, they are simply not attainable for an ordinary person, and this settles the issue altogether. However, in the presence of ressentiment-feelings, the disvalue of physical impotency is *not* admitted. It is even ennobled in the self-deception that they are sour. But — and this is the very "tragic" in all resentment feelings — *throughout the process of the emotional inversion of value-detraction and value-elevation there remains translucent, no matter how faintly, the true order of values and their ranks, in the background of the entire value-conflict.*

This simultaneous value detraction and elevation may be graphed in the following way, where "I" stands for the impotence in the feelings of ressentiment and "W" for the value detracted from its proper level:

2. In order to bring into focus the ranks that hold among values we must first look at some details of the nature of values themselves. This will provide us with a platform from which we can see the nature of value deceptions and value illusions which constantly plague all people charged with ressentiment.

What are values? There is a great deal of mention of values in present-day society. It seems that many people, more often than not in managerial or politically higher offices, believe that talking about values implies knowing already what they are. The talk about values was also fashionable in Germany during Scheler's lifetime. The determination of the nature of values also needed to be staked out, at that time as in ours today. It was one of the many lifelong areas of Scheler's pursuits, in glaring contrast, we must add, to the majority of twentieth-century philosophers who, like Heidegger, sometimes misconstrue entirely the nature of value-being by referring to only one or two classes of them. Being at the threshold of the twenty-first century, one can be pretty sure that twentieth-century philosophy will likely be characterized in the future by its conspicuous lack of research and concern into the being of values and the foundations of ethics.

First of all, values are given to us in feeling them. True, they can be thought of, and willed, but only after they have passed through feeling them. This is analogous to colors, says Scheler's, which can only be seen. Just as colors are given to us "in" seeing them, or sounds "in" hearing them, values are first given to us "in" feeling them. Note, however, that colors and sounds, like values, can also be present to thinking and observation. However, this is only pursuant to the respective primary acts of seeing, hearing, and feeling.

Feeling, on the other hand, is different from acts of seeing and hearing in that it does *not* occur exclusively in sense perception as seeing and hearing do. It is true that we can also feel a number of values with the senses, like pain given in the sense of touch. But feelings can be entirely *personal* also, in which cases they are not given in any of the five senses. Injustice, for instance, is felt in a personal feeling, not sensory feeling.

Furthermore, values are, like colors, *independent* of the things they belong to. The value "useful" may pertain to a piece of furniture or to a pen I am taking notes with, just as the vermilion of a rock fish may also be the color of a car. The independence values have of their substrates has far reaching consequences. Let it be mentioned only that the independence values have of things, and vice versa, is an ontological basis for all negotiable values in economics, for example, those negotiated in a stock-market. In this regard, the independence holding between values and things is itself rather useful for human beings who want to pursue technical as well as technological aims, etc.

But said independence has also unfortunate effects in society. In society, values are believed to be mostly quantifiable. Their quantifiability is used to bring them under control mechanisms, such as in programs designed to stem inflation, in order that acceptable value conditions can be sustained. We can without difficulty see at this point that the controllability of quantifiable values is based in their independence of things. This state of affairs makes it possible for the global human household (economics) to be kept in relative order, or not.

The excessive use of quantifiable values in modern society implies the forbidding tendency to look at the entire realm of values, including values which are not at all quantifiable, as manageable values. The value of persons itself, which is not quantifiable, has become subject to being reduced to quantifiable work hours and success. In such cases, not only is the unique self-value of an individual person ignored, but also the *entire* realm of values is subordinated to quantification. The education of children is, unfortunately, no exception to this value-deception, because education is largely seen to be effective first if there is enough money for it available. The dedicated teacher is subsumed under this contortion of a cultural value.

Scheler foresaw this untimely development and to counter it he tried to bring into bold relief the *dignity* and unique value of the individual person. He stressed that the concept of "person" is totally indifferent to race, gender, ethnicity, wealth, or individual beliefs. And he suspected there to be a stealthy societal resentment creeping among those who lack fullness of personality but compensate their hollow selves by judging others by the quantity of their work and success, all independent of social stations. It is therefore false to assume that only socially disadvantaged persons can suffer from ressentiment. There is a tragic lack of love in society. Indeed, at the end of the text before us, Scheler charges society with quantifying the most precious quality human beings have, love itself, in that love of the individual person is being replaced by a quantified love for humanity expressed in fund-raisings. The value of individual and undivided samaritan love of the other — for the sake of which the young Scheler turned as a teenager toward Catholicism (his mother was Jewish, his father Lutheran) — is giving way to a false humanitarianism.

Both the value-independence and the givenness of values in feelings we just discussed suggest that values have criteria of rankings. Before we list the value-ranks, we wish to mention some criteria which are indices for the heights and levels these ranks have among each other. The criteria of the heights of values run through all ranks. They are:

1. The higher a value-rank is, the less its values are divisible and controllable, and the less they depend on material.
2. The higher a value-rank is, the more it lasts in time.
3. The higher a value-rank is, the less its values can be willed and managed.
4. The higher a value-rank is, the more its values generate personal contentment, happiness, and inner peace.

All valuations we make in our lives are applicable to these criteria. Values themselves divide into five *spectral* value-ranks. Like individual values themselves, the five value-ranks themselves, too, have an analogy to colorations, because colorations, too, rest on a few ranks of spectral colors, without which there cannot be colorations of things.

The five value-ranks are not specifically treated in the present text, but underlie it all the way through. They are treated in detail in Scheler's aforementioned *Formalism in Ethics and Non-Formal Ethics of Values*, and his essay "Ordo Amoris." In chapters III, IV, and V of the present text some of them are seen in light of ressentiment feelings.

Starting with the lowest rank and continuing in ascending order, the ranks of values are as follows:

The lowest rank contains all values given in tactile feelings of the body. They range from the value of bodily "comfort" down to "discomfort." We share these values with animals but, according to the independence values have of their substrates, what is comfortable to one species may not be so for another, and what is comfortable to one individual is not necessarily comfortable to another.

The next higher rank ranges from the value of "useful" down to the negative value of "not useful." These are pragmatic values and are connected with things, work, and anything expedient, as the Greek word "pragma" suggests. They also pertain to technology as the Greek word "techne," meaning "cunning of hand," "craft," "art," suggests. We also share these values with animals, for example, when birds are building their nests trying to find the most useful material for this. But with humans the pragmatic value-rank encompasses much more. It spans the usefulness of the atom and the exploration of outer space. The emotive preferring of the values of these two lowest ranks, i.e., leaning toward them over higher ones, is rampant in a society typified by an excessive cultivation of the human body and utility values. These excesses are reflected in exorbitant sums of money and time spent annually in industrialized nations for sports, entertainment, tools, and gadgets, amounting to an international multi-billion dollar industry. The preference of the two lowest value-ranks is unfortunate in comparison to the modest funds available for cultural values like global education, the arts, and equal distribution of nutrition on our planet, something Scheler regarded as one of the highest priorities of moral behavior in person-to-person love. He once referred to the preference of the lower two ranks over all others as the deceiving "star of society."

What distinguishes the two lower value-ranks from all other ranks is also their localizability in organs and things. Discomfort of body pain is as localizable as is a thing's usefulness.

The next higher rank contains "life values" in two ways: They either pertain to the function and appearance of life and nature, on the one hand, or to human heroism, on the other. They range from the value of "noble" down to "deficient" or "bad." A knight riding a horse, or an old oak tree, have a noble aura about them, whereas the appearance of a pragmatic thing like a computer does not. The life values inherent in heroic actions must serve at least in part the preservation of life. What distinguishes the rank of life-values from the former two lower ranks is that they are not localizable. They spread through an entire organism as do health, fatigue, and feelings of oncoming death; or the nobility of a heroic action is not a part of such action but suffuses it from its beginning to its end and beyond its presence. According to the order thus far given, it is not surprising that for Scheler life values of agriculture and environment are higher than both pragmatic technological and sensible values.

The fourth highest rank contains mental and cultural values given only to the person. There are three kinds of them: Aesthetic values, which encompass the values of "beautiful" down to "ugly," legal values of "right" and "wrong," and the value of the "cognition of truth."

The highest value-rank spans the "holy" and "unholy." Its values, too, can only be felt by a person.

3. This brings us to the third component in the emotive structure of ressentiment. All ressentiment feelings necessitate active or passive intersubjective acts of "comparing" with others, in particular with those who have no ressentiment feelings.

In this regard, an important factor concerning the phenomenology of intersubjective experience, commonly referred to as the problem of the "I" and the "Thou," should be mentioned here. In phenomenological discussions the role of acts of comparing with others is rarely, if at all, seen in its significance. It appears that in pertinent literature authored by such thinkers as M. Buber, E. Husserl, and E. Levinas among many others, little or no mention is made on the *constitutive* role of passively and actively comparing ourselves with others. Whether or not there is intersubjective ressentiment present, comparing lies at the very root of *any* intersubjective experience. Indeed, it can be held that without it no co-experience of a person with another person can occur.

Comparing is independent of whether my ego presupposes the presence of an alter-ego, a position held by Scheler since 1913, or whether an alter-ego presupposes an ego, something which E. Husserl suggested.

Comparing with others is at the root of each alternative. It appears that the significance of comparing was first seen by I. Kant in his essay, "Mutmasslicher Anfang der Menschengeschichte," (The Probable Beginning of Human History). Kant states here that the first "stirrings" of reason consisted in making "comparisons" between objects given to the nutritive drive, on the one hand, with those not given to this drive, on the other, e.g., with visible but inedible objects. Comparing, says Kant, provoked enlargement of knowledge in that the first human beings were "renegades" from the spells of natural drives which drove them to "toy with the nature's voice." Comparing, Kant goes on to say, pushed the first humans to the "rim of an abyss" and into an eternity which, in turn, made them free. Both reason and freedom, therefore, are born together and in conjunction with the first act of comparing.

Specifically, a person filled with ressentiment is provoked to compare his weakened value-feelings with those of persons having no ressentiment. This is the reason why the ressentiment-subject can elevate the values of his powerlessness. He even gets an aberrated satisfaction by emotively elevating negative values to a more praiseworthy level, but where they do not belong. He remains, as we indicated earlier, faced with the unattainability of those values that his ressentiment feeling keeps on tussling with in vain and which he detracts on a lower, less praiseworthy level. Ressentiment feelings just do not cease to be encapsuled within an emotive comparison between "elevation" of inferior and negative values and the emotive failure to completely deprecate unattainable, positive values.

Intersubjective comparing also bears heavily on the nature of society itself. A society beset with social discrepancies and competition is a most fertile ground for the psychic venom of ressentiment with its value-deceptions to seep into all walks of life. The opposite of this holds when individuals freely accept the social stations they are born in and where there is little or no competition. The pervasive slavery in ancient Rome, for example, apparently did not generate as much ressentiment against Roman masters as we would expect. To be born a slave at the time was felt to be a natural state. Neither Aristotle in his *Nicomachean Ethics,* nor Plato in his *Republic* perceive an omen of possible upheavals when they touch upon the theme of social classes. Accepting the social bed one was born in was, right or wrong, the order of the day, and contributed to some communal feelings of solidarity which modern societies are not prone to develop.

By contrast, any group which neither freely accepts different social levels nor individual persons of higher stations will — as in a competitive society — be haunted by ressentiment. For this reason, the intensity of active comparing with others is especially obvious in the competition of contemporary society. Dishing out a myriad of awards — a symbol of competition — for whatever reason, and sometimes even for insignificant so-called accomplishments, has turned into an all but a cosmetic practice. The intensity of competition lets awards mushroom everywhere and for almost anything, sometimes for such oddities as the worst movie or ugliest grimace of the year. One can even apply for and buy awards. They are supposed to make an awardee comfortable; yet others, like ressentiment-subjects, to be sure, remain less comfortable. In many walks of life including business, awards are given with a tacit psychological motivation to spur others to emulate the "role models" and thus to encourage more productivity.

Scheler gives a salient example for competitive feelings of resentment based in a psychic impotency by mentioning a type of person he calls the "arrivist" (der Streber). The arrivist is a person who incessantly tries to "arrive" at the top, outdoing his fellow persons at any cost. This person-type comes close to certain "overachievers" today. He is unable to love, to give and forgive, to sacrifice, to admit defeat with his head up, to make friends, to be content with his own self. He is impotent to enjoy the value and quality of his life. He is good at smirking rather than smiling in friendship. Impervious and sometimes stiff as his personality is, his motivation to do extra work and to crave for perfection is not motivated by realizing a common good like that of a corporation, a company, nation, or church. Rather, his impotency to fill the deep gaps in his hollow personality generates the constant urge to do better than, and win over others *in public* and to fish for social esteem and respect. Marks for excellence acquired in school, business, or elsewhere, cover up the personal dearth which makes him a social loner rather than a friend, sharing and feeling compassion.

In society material overachievement also plays into applied ethics, so called, which tries to seek solutions for such moral dilemmas as abortion, racketeering, euthanasia, cruelty to animals, substitute motherhood, cloning genes, and many more moral problems: solutions cannot keep up with the fast pace of technology from which they in part originate. One avoids asking what this ethics is applied "from." And there is its impotency. Applied ethics — like business ethics, legal ethics, or medical ethics, or ethics for nursing or for the police, even "ethics committees" — are indispensable for perceiving relevant states of affairs but appear to be impotent to encourage individual inspection into the moral tenor of the *individual person*. Instead, applied ethics favors seeking solutions for societal dilemmas by open debate alone. There is nothing wrong with this as long as we have recourse to the philosophical foundations of professional ethics is, for example, those provided by Aristotle, Kant, or Mill. Applied ethics not infrequently presupposes that if one is able to turn society as a whole around for the better and to improve its political institutions and legal systems, the individual, too, will, in turn, also become good. But all careful investigations into the foundations of ethics have shown that the very opposite is the case: namely, that it is first the individual person's moral self-inspection, improvement of his actions, careful cultivation of *self*-responsibility, and love for others that will improve a society, its institutions, and its legal systems. It is easy to shift blame away from oneself, a point Scheler makes in order to indicate there may be blatant but hidden ressentiment. Likewise, it is easy for an arrivist to work for any goal but for that of his own moral standing. Whenever an individual is unable to face himself and instead loses himself and dissolves into external, societal relations to elude himself, there is an index of ressentiment possible. Scheler alluded to this in 1913 as "alienation" (Entfremdung).

Having explained the three components of the structure of ressentiment (1) the emotive detraction of positive values, (2) the ranks among values, and (3) intersubjective comparing, there is no further need to analyze the various instances of ressentiment Scheler offers in his investigation.

But two technical remarks may be added here instead, before reading the text. The first pertains to the initial forms of resentment Scheler mentions and which merge into ressentiment proper when the above given structure is at hand. These initial forms of ressentiment are: revenge, malice, envy, spite, "Scheelsucht" and "Schadenfreude." The two latter German words, ask for some explanation because there are no adequate English equivalents for them.

German "Scheelsucht" refers to an uninterrupted blind impulse to detract. When people deride classical music, or rock music, because they have no appreciation of either, there is not necessarily ressentiment involved but likes or dislikes. But when someone derides *anything* he comes across, there is a blind value detraction present. There is neither a particular object, nor a particular class of objects around this person which is not subject to his derision. He suffers from a plain, continued obsession to detract and to belittle the value of anything whatever, indeed that of the whole world. If, however, the latter is the case, such a person may turn desperate; in very intense cases of this kind a person may become suicidal. The word "Scheelsucht" is hardly used in German parlance. But its literal meaning fits well with all that has been said. The more common adjective of the noun "Scheelsucht" is: "scheel," which means "cross-eyed." And "scheelsuechtig" means to have a very strong need to look askance at others, to disparage. In our context, then, the word would figuratively translate into being "cross-valued" in the sense of the above mentioned inversion of value detraction and value elevation.

The word "Schadenfreude," on the other hand, is sometimes used in English, and refers to reveling in someone else's bad luck and misfortune. For example, the disappointed fans of a badly losing basketball team may suddenly revel over an unanticipated streak of bad luck that befalls the opposing team as it tries in vain to end the game and then ends up losing the game.

The second technical remark pertains to the German Collected Edition of Scheler's philosophy: the *Gesammelte Werke*. Presently, it comprises fourteen volumes, published from 1954 to 1965 by Francke Verlag, Bern, Switzerland; and from 1986 on by Bouvier Verlag, Bonn, Germany. From 1954 to 1969 Max Scheler's widow, Maria Scheler, was its editor, and from 1970 on, the present writer has borne undivided responsibility for the edition.

An up-to-date list of English translations of Scheler's works is contained in: Max Scheler. *On Feeling, Knowing, and Valuing*. Edited with an Introduction by Harold J. Bershady. The University of Chicago Press, Chicago, London, 1992.

Manfred S. Frings
DePaul University, Chicago

It is one thing to sift the data of inner observation conceptually and to set them up as compounds, then to decompose these into ultimate "simple" elements and to study, through artificial variation by observation and experiment, the conditions and results of such combinations. It is quite another to describe and understand the units of experience and meaning which are contained in the totality of man's life itself and have not merely been created by an artificial process of "division" and "synthesis." The first method, influenced by the natural sciences, is that of a synthetic-constructive psychology which wants to *explain*. The second method characterizes an analytic and descriptive psychology which wants to *understand*.[1] The former operates with artificially created mental units. Therefore these units need not be encompassed and apprehended by any one act of experience — their component parts can pertain to completely different acts of experience. For instance, the sense perceptions which are simultaneously in my mind at this very moment belong to fundamentally different units of experience — for example, to the perception of the writing paper, to my sitting on my chair, to the experience that I am in this room, that I am writing, etc. Nevertheless I can unite them at will into combinations or analyze such combinations into parts. There may also be many processes which genetically determine one another, but which I do not experience and whose occurrence can only be established by comparative causal considerations with artificially varied initial and final terms. For example, my attitude and feeling equilibrium stems from normal sensations in my ear which correspond to the sense of equilibrium of the statolith located there. In an analogous way, the sensations and reproductions of sensations which may, for example, go into the perception of a book lying before me are not part of one unit of experience. The factual presence of these elements does not prevent them from being excluded from the unified experience of this perception. On the other hand, mental data which are extremely complex in terms of the first procedure may nevertheless be phenomenally *simple,* for they may be given in *one* act of experience. If so, they are "phenomenologically simple." A friendship I experienced, a love, an insult, an overall attitude toward my environment in a phase of my childhood — all these will contain combinations of the most heterogenous partial contents (sensations, representations, conclusions, judgments, acts of love and hatred, feelings, moods, etc.), viewed in the first perspective. Moreover, these elements are distributed among completely different points of objective time and are interrupted by experiential units of an entirely different nature and unity, as well as by sleeping, waking, illness, etc. Yet they form phenomenal units of experience which I feel to be active (not as objective causes) and which are instrumental in determining my actions. It is true that I can once more dissect each of these units into smaller subunits — into some "event" or "situation," into a particular look or smile of my friend, etc. But these partial units must always receive their meaning and unity through one act of experience, not through an artificial separation and synthesis. Even as parts, they remain experienced partial units; they can never be constructed components. The units and compounds at which the two methods arrive can never correspond, nor can their respective results coincide. Their ultimate philosophical relation does not concern us here.

It is the purpose of this essay to examine *ressentiment* as one such unit of experience and action.

We do not use the word *"ressentiment"* because of a special predilection for the French language, but because we did not succeed in translating it into German. Moreover, Nietzsche has made it a *terminus technicus.* In the natural meaning of the French word I detect two elements. First of all, *ressentiment* is the repeated experiencing and reliving of a particular emotional response reaction against someone else. The continual reliving of the emotion sinks it more deeply into the center of the personality, but concomitantly removes it from the person's zone of action and expression. It is not a mere intellectual recollection of the emotion and of the events to which it "responded" — it is a re-experiencing of the emotion itself, a renewal of the original feeling.[2] Secondly, the word implies that the quality of this emotion is negative, i.e., that it contains a movement of hostility. Perhaps the German word *"Groll"* (rancor) comes closest to the essential meaning of the term. "Rancor" is just such a suppressed wrath, independent of the ego's activity, which moves obscurely through the mind. It finally takes shape through the repeated reliving of intentionalities of hatred or other hostile emotions. In itself it does not contain a specific hostile intention, but it nourishes any number of such intentions.[3]

# ON THE PHENOMENOLOGY AND
## SOCIOLOGY OF *Ressentiment*

Among the scanty discoveries which have been made in recent times about the origin of moral judgments, Friedrich Nietzsche's discovery that *ressentiment* can be the source of such value judgments is the most profound. This remains true even if his specific characterization of Christian love as the most delicate "flower of *ressentiment*" should turn out to be mistaken.

"But *this* is the event: out of the stem of that tree of revenge and hatred, of Jewish hatred — the most profound and sublime of all, the hatred which creates ideals and transforms values and which has never had its like on earth — there grew something equally incomparable, a *new love,* the most profound and sublime kind of love: — and indeed from what other stem could it have grown? ... But let us not think that it grew as the negation of that thirst for revenge, as the antithesis of Jewish hatred! No, the reverse is true! This love grew from it as its crown, as the triumphant crown unfolding ever more broadly in the purest brightness and solar plenitude. In the lofty realm of light, so to speak, it aimed at the goals of that hatred, at victory, booty, seduction — with the same urge which made the roots of that hatred dig more and more thoroughly and covetously into whatever had depth and was evil. This Jesus of Nazareth, as the living Gospel of Love, this "Savior" who brought bliss and victory to the poor, the sick, the sinners — did he not represent seduction in its most sinister and most irresistible form, seduction and a detour to precisely those *Jewish* values and innovations of the ideal? Is it not true that Israel has reached the final aim of its sublime vindictiveness through this 'Savior,' this seeming adversary and destroyer of Israel?" *(Genealogy of Morals,* Part I, Section 8).

"The slave revolt in morality begins when *ressentiment* itself becomes creative and produces values: the *ressentiment* of beings to whom the real reaction, that of the deed, is denied, who can only indulge in imaginary revenge. Whereas every noble morality springs from a triumphant acceptance and affirmation of oneself, slave morality is in its very essence a negation of everything 'outside' and 'different,' of whatever is 'not oneself': and *this* negation is its creative deed. This reversal of the perspective of valuation — this necessary determination by the outside rather than by oneself — is typical of *ressentiment:* in order to arise, slave morality always needs a hostile external world. Physiologically speaking, it needs external stimuli in order to act at all — its action is fundamentally a reaction." (Part I, Section 10).

— "I see nothing, I hear all the more. It is a cautious, a gentle and insidious muttering and whispering in all nooks and corners. It seems to me that they are lying; a sugary mildness sticks to every sound. Weakness is to be made a *merit,* there can be no doubt — it is as you said" —

— "Go on!"

— "and impotence, inability to retaliate, is to become 'goodness'; timorous lowliness becomes 'humility'; submission to those whom one hates is 'obedience' (obedience toward one of whom they say that he decrees this submission — they call him God). The inoffensiveness of the weak, even the cowardice in which he is rich, his unavoidable obligation to wait at the door acquires a good name, as 'patience,' it is also called virtue; the inability to avenge oneself is supposed to be a voluntary renunciation of revenge, sometimes it is even called forgiveness ('for *they* know not what they do — we alone know what *they* do'!). They also speak of 'love for one's enemies,' — and they sweat while doing so." (Part I, Section 14).

These are the chief passages in which Friedrich Nietzsche develops his remarkable thesis. For the moment, let us ignore the relation of *ressentiment* to Christian values in order to penetrate more deeply into the *unit of experience* designated by the term.

Instead of defining the word, let us briefly characterize or describe the phenomenon. *Ressentiment* is a self-poisoning of the mind which has quite definite causes and consequences. It is a lasting mental attitude, caused by the systematic repression of certain emotions and affects which, as such, are normal components of human nature. Their repression leads to the constant tendency to indulge in certain kinds of value delusions and corresponding value judgments. The emotions and affects primarily concerned are revenge, hatred, malice, envy, the impulse to detract, and spite.[1]

Thirst for revenge is the most important source of *ressentiment*. As we have seen, the very term *"ressentiment"* indicates that we have to do with reactions which presuppose the previous apprehension of another person's state of mind. The desire for revenge — in contrast with all active and aggressive impulses, be they friendly or hostile — is also such a reactive impulse. It is always preceded by an attack or an injury. Yet it must be clearly distinguished from the impulse for reprisals or self-defense, even when this reaction is accompanied by anger, fury, or indignation. If an animal bites its attacker, this cannot be called "revenge." Nor does an immediate reprisal against a box on the ear fall under this heading. Revenge is distinguished by two essential characteristics. First of all, the immediate reactive impulse, with the accompanying emotions of anger and rage, is temporarily or at least momentarily checked and restrained, and the response is consequently postponed to a later time and to a more suitable occasion ("just wait till next time"). This blockage is caused by the reflection that an immediate reaction would lead to defeat, and by a concomitant pronounced feeling of "inability" and "impotence." Thus even revenge as such, based as it is upon an experience of impotence, is always primarily a matter of those who are "weak" in some respect. Furthermore, it is of the essence of revenge that it always contains the *consciousness* of "tit for tat," so that it is never a mere emotional reaction?[2]

These two characteristics make revenge the most suitable source for the formation of *ressentiment*. The nuances of language are precise. There is a progression of feeling which starts with revenge and runs via rancor, envy, and impulse to detract all the way to spite, coming close to *ressentiment*. Usually, revenge and envy still have specific objects. They do not arise without special reasons and are directed against definite objects, so that they do not outlast their motives. The desire for revenge disappears when vengeance has been taken, when the person against whom it was directed has been punished or has punished himself, or when one truly forgives him. In the same way, envy vanishes when the envied possession becomes ours. The impulse to detract, however, is not in the same sense tied to definite objects — it does not arise through specific causes with which it disappears. On the contrary, this affect *seeks* those objects, those aspects of men and things, from which it can draw gratification. It likes to disparage and to smash pedestals, to dwell on the negative aspects of excellent men and things, exulting in the fact that such faults are more perceptible through their contrast with the strongly positive qualities. Thus there is set a fixed pattern of experience which can accommodate the most diverse contents. This form or structure fashions each concrete experience of life and selects it from possible experiences. The impulse to detract, therefore, is no mere result of such an experience, and the experience will arise regardless of considerations whether its object could in any way, directly or indirectly, further or hamper the individual concerned. In "spite," this impulse has become even more profound and deep-seated — it is, as it were, always ready to burst forth and to betray itself in an unbridled gesture, a way of smiling, etc. An analogous road leads from simple *Schadenfreude* to "malice." The latter, more detached than the former from *definite* objects, tries to bring about ever new opportunities for *Schadenfreude*.

Yet all this is not *ressentiment*. These are only stages in the development of its sources. Revenge, envy, the impulse to detract, spite, *Schadenfreude*, and malice lead to *ressentiment* only if there occurs neither a moral self-conquest (such as *genuine* forgiveness in the case of revenge) nor an act or some other adequate expression of emotion (such as verbal abuse or shaking one's fist), and if this restraint is caused by a pronounced awareness of impotence. There will be no *ressentiment* if he who thirsts for revenge really acts and avenges himself, if he who is consumed by hatred harms his enemy, gives him "a piece of his mind," or even merely vents his spleen in the presence of others. Nor will the envious fall under the dominion of *ressentiment* if he seeks to acquire the envied possession by means of work, barter, crime, or violence. *Ressentiment* can only arise if these emotions are particularly powerful and yet must be suppressed because they are coupled with the feeling that one is unable to act them out — either because of weakness, physical or mental, or because of fear. Through its very origin, *ressentiment* is therefore chiefly confined to those who *serve* and are *dominated* at the moment, who fruitlessly resent the sting of authority. When it occurs elsewhere, it is either due to psychological contagion — and the spiritual venom of *ressentiment* is extremely contagious — or to the violent suppression of an impulse which subsequently revolts by "embittering" and "poisoning" the personality. If an ill-treated servant can vent his spleen in the antechamber, he will remain free from the inner venom of *ressentiment,* but it will engulf him if he must hide his feelings and keep his negative and hostile emotions to himself.

But let us examine the various sources of *ressentiment* more closely.

Impulses of revenge lead to *ressentiment* the more they change into actual *vindictiveness,* the more their direction shifts toward indeterminate groups of objects which need only share one common characteristic, and the less they are satisfied by vengeance taken on a specific object. If the desire for revenge remains permanently unsatisfied, and especially if the feeling of "being right" (lacking in an outburst of rage, but an integral part of revenge) is intensified into the idea of a "duty," the individual may actually wither away and die.[3] The vindictive person is instinctively and without a conscious act of volition drawn toward events which may give rise to vengefulness, or he tends to see injurious intentions in all kinds of perfectly innocent actions and remarks of others. Great touchiness is indeed frequently a symptom of a vengeful character. The vindictive person is always in search of objects, and in fact he attacks — in the belief that he is simply wreaking vengeance. This vengeance restores his damaged feeling of personal value, his injured "honor," or it brings "satisfaction" for the wrongs he has endured. When it is repressed, vindictiveness leads to *ressentiment,* a process which is intensified when the *imagination* of vengeance, too, is repressed — and finally the very emotion of revenge itself. Only then does this *state of mind* become associated with the tendency to detract from the other person's value, which brings an illusory easing of the tension.

The following factors contribute to strengthen these preconditions:

The desire for revenge, which is itself caused by a repression, has powerful repressive tendencies. This is expressed in the saying that "revenge is a dish which should be taken cold." Everything else being equal, it is therefore always the attitude of the weaker party. But at the same time, the injured person always places himself on the same level as his injurer.[4] A slave who has a slavish nature and accepts his status does not desire revenge when he is injured by his master; nor does a servile servant who is reprimanded or a child that is slapped. Conversely, feelings of revenge are favored by strong pretensions which remain concealed, or by great pride coupled with an inadequate social position. There follows the important sociological law that this psychological dynamite will spread with the *discrepancy* between the political, constitutional, or traditional status of a group and its *factual* power. It is the difference between these two factors which is decisive, not one of them alone. Social *ressentiment,* at least, would be slight in a democracy which is not only political, but also social and tends toward equality of property. But the same would be the case — and *was* the case — in a caste society such as that of India, or in a society with sharply divided classes. *Ressentiment* must therefore be strongest in a society like ours, where approximately equal rights (political and otherwise) or formal social equality, publicly recognized, go hand in hand with wide factual differences in power, property, and education. While each has the "right" to compare himself with everyone else, he cannot do so in fact. Quite independently of the characters and experiences of individuals, a potent charge of *ressentiment* is here accumulated by the very *structure of society.*

We must add the fact that revenge tends to be transformed into *ressentiment* the more it is directed against lasting situations which are felt to be "injurious" but beyond one's control — in other words, the more the injury is experienced as a destiny. This will be most pronounced when a person or group feels that the very fact and quality of its *existence* is a matter which calls for revenge. For an individual, a case in point would be a physical or other natural defect, especially one that is easily visible. The *ressentiment* of cripples or of people of subnormal intelligence is a well-known phenomenon. Jewish *ressenti-*

*ment,* which Nietzsche rightly designates as enormous, finds double nourishment: first in the discrepancy between the colossal national pride of "the chosen people" and a contempt and discrimination which weighed on them for centuries like a destiny, and in modern times through the added discrepancy between formal constitutional equality and factual discrimination. Certainly the extremely powerful acquisitive instinct of this people is due — over and beyond natural propensities and other causes — to a deep-rooted disturbance of Jewish self-confidence. It is an overcompensation for the lack of a social acknowledgment which would satisfy the national self-esteem. In the development of the labor movement, the conviction that the very existence and fate of the proletariat "cries for revenge" also became a mighty dynamic factor. The more a permanent social pressure is felt to be a "fatality," the less it can free forces for the practical transformation of these conditions, and the more it will lead to indiscriminate *criticism* without any positive aims. This peculiar kind of *"ressentiment* criticism" is characterized by the fact that improvements in the conditions criticized cause no satisfaction — they merely cause discontent, for they destroy the growing pleasure afforded by invective and negation. Many modern political parties will be extremely annoyed by a partial satisfaction of their demands or by the constructive participation of their representatives in public life, for such participation mars the delight of oppositionism. It is peculiar to *"ressentiment* criticism" that it does not seriously desire that its demands be fulfilled. It does not want to cure the evil: the evil is merely a pretext for the criticism. We all know certain representatives in our parliaments whose criticism is absolute and uninhibited, precisely because they count on never being ministers. Only when this *aversion* from power (in contrast with the *will* to power) becomes a permanent trait, is criticism moved by *ressenti-ment.* Conversely, it is an old experience that the political criticism of a party loses its pungency when this party becomes positively associated with the authority of the state.[5]

Another source of *ressentiment* lies in *envy, jealousy,* and the *competitive urge.* *"Envy,"* as the term is understood in everyday usage, is due to a feeling of impotence which we experience when another person owns a good we covet. But this tension between desire and nonfulfillment does not lead to envy until it flares up into hatred against the owner, until the latter is falsely considered to be the *cause* of our privation. Our factual inability to acquire a good is wrongly interpreted as a positive action *against* our desire[6] — a delusion which diminishes the original tension. Both the experience of impotence and the causal delusion are essential preconditions of true envy. If we are merely displeased that another person owns a good, this can be an incentive for acquiring it through work, purchase, violence, or robbery. *Envy* occurs when we fail in doing so and feel powerless. Therefore it is a great error to think that envy — along with covetousness, ambition, and vanity — is a motive force in the development of civilization. Envy does not strengthen the acquisitive urge; it weakens it. It leads to *ressentiment* when the coveted values are such as cannot be acquired and lie in the sphere in which we compare ourselves to others. The most powerless envy is also the most terrible. Therefore *existential envy,* which is directed against the other person's very *nature,* is the strongest source of *ressentiment.* It is as if it whispers continually: "I can forgive everything, but not that you *are* — that you are *what* you are — that I am not what you are — indeed that I am not *you.*" This form of envy strips the opponent of his very existence, for this existence as such is felt to be a "pressure," a "reproach," and an unbearable humiliation. In the lives of great men there are always critical periods of instability, in which they alternately envy and try to love those whose merits they cannot but esteem. Only gradually, one of these attitudes will predominate. Here lies the meaning of Goethe's reflection that "against another's great merits, there is no remedy but love."[7] In his *Torquato Tasso* (Act II, Scene 3) he suggests that Antonio's relations with Tasso are characterized by this kind of ambiguity. An analogous dynamic situation is seen between Marius and Sulla, Caesar and Brutus. Besides these cases of existential envy, which are rare, the innate characteristics of groups of individuals (beauty, racial excellence, hereditary character traits) are the chief causes of *ressentiment* envy. These types of envy are the only ones which entail that illusory devaluation of the envied values which will be discussed further down.

In all these cases, the origin of *ressentiment* is connected with a tendency to make comparisons between others and oneself. This attitude requires a brief examination. Each of us — noble or common, good or evil — continually compares his own value with that of others.

If I choose a model, a "hero," I am somehow tied to such a comparison. All jealousy, all ambition, and even an ideal like the "imitation of Christ" is full of such comparisons. We cannot agree with Georg Simmel, who says that the "noble man" refuses to compare himself to anyone. A man who refuses any comparison is not noble, but an "oddity" in the Goethean sense, a "unique buffoon," or perhaps a snob. Yet Simmel has the right thing in mind. A comparison can be conceived in different ways. The two terms of a relation may be apprehended separately, prior to and independently of any comparison or other relation (such as "similarity" or "identity"). Conversely, the perception of the terms may be the actualization of a previously apprehended but still indeterminate relation. It is a proven phenomenal fact that the relation between two terms (for example, colors, sounds, faces, etc.) can be contained in the perception of one of these terms alone. Thus we may be struck by the particular resemblance of one face to another which yet we cannot picture, but have to seek in our memory. The awareness of a relation here determines the conscious appearance of the second term. There is, indeed, phenomenal proof that there are pure experiences of relatedness, which select and actualize their terms only afterwards. The specific contents then come to occupy the still indeterminate places of a previously given relation. These distinctions are important here. The attitude which Simmel calls "nobility" is distinguished by the fact that the comparison of values, the "measuring" of my own value as against that of another person, is never the constitutive *precondition* for apprehending either. Moreover, the values are always apprehended in their entirety, not only in certain selected aspects. The "noble person" has a completely naive and non-reflective awareness of his own value and of his fullness of being, an obscure conviction which enriches every conscious moment of his existence, as if he were autonomously rooted in the universe. This should not be mistaken for "pride." Quite on the contrary, pride results from an experienced *diminution* of this "naive" self-confidence. It is a way of "holding on" to one's value, of seizing and "preserving" it deliberately.[8] The noble man's naive self-confidence, which is as natural to him as tension is to the muscles, permits him calmly to assimilate the merits of others in all the fullness of their substance and configuration. He never "grudges" them their merits. On the contrary: he rejoices in their virtues and feels that they make the world more worthy of love. His naive self-confidence is by no means "compounded" of a series of positive valuations based on specific qualities, talents, and virtues: it is originally directed at his very essence and being. Therefore he can afford to admit that another person has certain "qualities" superior to his own or is more "gifted" in some respects — indeed in all respects. Such a conclusion does not diminish his naive awareness of his own value, which needs no justification or proof by achievements or abilities. Achievements merely serve to confirm it. On the other hand, the "common" man (in the exact acceptation of the term) can only experience his value and that of another if he relates the two, and he clearly perceives only those qualities which constitute possible differences. The noble man experiences value *prior to* any comparison, the common man *in* and *through* a comparison. For the latter, the relation is the selective precondition for apprehending *any* value. Every value is a relative thing, "higher" or "lower," "more" or "less" than his own. He arrives at value judgments by comparing himself to others and others to himself.

Two different human types share in this basic attitude, for it can go together with either strength or weakness, power or impotence. The energetic variety of the "common" man becomes an *arriviste,* the weak variety becomes the *man of ressentiment.*[9]

An *arriviste* is not a man who energetically and potently pursues power, property, honor, and other values. He does not deserve this name as long as he still thinks in terms of the intrinsic value of something which he actively furthers and represents by profession or calling. The ultimate goal of the *arriviste's* aspirations is not to acquire a thing of value, but to be more highly esteemed than others. He merely uses the "thing" as an indifferent occasion for overcoming the oppressive feeling of inferiority which results from his constant comparisons.

If this type of value experience comes to dominate a whole society, then the "system of free competition" will become the soul of this society. This system is in its "purest" form when the comparison transcends such specific spheres as classes or "estates," with their fixed customs and ways of living. The medieval peasant prior to the 13th century does not compare himself to the feudal lord, nor does the artisan compare himself to the knight. The peasant may make comparisons with respect to the richer more respected peasant, and in the same way everyone confines himself to his own sphere. Each group had its exclusive task in life, its objective unity of purpose. Thus every comparison took place within a strictly circumscribed frame of reference. At the most, these frames of reference could be compared in their totality. Therefore such periods are dominated by the idea that everyone has his "place" which has been assigned to him by God and nature and in which he has his personal duty to fulfill. His value consciousness and his aspirations never go beyond this sphere. From the king down to the hangman and the prostitute, everyone is "noble" in the sense that he considers himself as irreplaceable. In the "system of free competition," on the other hand, the notions on life's tasks and their value are not fundamental, they are but secondary derivations of the desire of all to surpass all the others. No "place" is more than a transitory point in this universal chase. The aspirations are intrinsically *boundless,* for they are no longer tied to any particular object or quality. The objects have become "commodities," destined for exchange and defined by their monetary value.[10] The progression of time is interpreted as "progress," and a specific "desire for progress" goes with this way of thinking. The "possession" or "enjoyment" of some unit of qualitative value used to be the end point of every economic motivation which forms a phenomenal unit of experience, great or small. Money, as a means of exchange, was only a transitional goal. Now, however, the final aim is a *quantity* of monetary value, and it is the quality of the commodity which has become a mere "transitional goal." The structure of the motivation, which used to be commodity —> money —> commodity, is now money —> commodity —> money (Karl Marx). Of course we can still enjoy qualitative values, but our enjoyment — and indeed its very possibility — is now limited to those objects which are most immediately recognized as units of commodity value.

There is a parallel tendency in the evaluation of the different *phases of life* (childhood, youth, maturity, old age). Not one of these phases has retained its own particular value and its peculiar significance. We are only aware of the *surplus* value which one phase may have as compared to the other. The ideas of "progress" and "regression" are not drawn from an empirical observation of the phases of life as such

— they are selective yardsticks which we apply to ourselves, to others, and to history. Jean-Jacques Rousseau was the first to protest against the pedagogical theories which consider childhood and youth as mere precursors of maturity. Leopold von Ranke rejected the childish liberal belief in historical progress in the following magnificent sentences: "Such a 'mediated' generation would have no significance of its own. It would only be important as a stepping-stone toward the next generation, and it would have no direct relation to the divine. However, I affirm that every epoch is directly related to God, and its value does not lie in what it engenders, but in its very existence, in its own self."[11] The desire for progress corresponds to the view rejected by Ranke, for it has no definite objective goals. It is activated by nothing but the wish to surpass a given phase, to set a "record," and the specific goals are only *secondary consequences* of this desire and indifferent "transitional points" in the movement of progress.

The case is different when the bent towards relative valuation is accompanied by *impotence*. Then the oppressive sense of inferiority which always goes with the "common" attitude cannot lead to active behavior. Yet the painful tension demands relief. This is afforded by the specific *value delusion of ressentiment*. To relieve the tension, the common man seeks a feeling of superiority or equality, and he attains his purpose by an illusory *devaluation* of the other man's qualities or by a specific "blindness" to these qualities. But secondly — and here lies the main achievement of *ressentiment* — he falsities the *values themselves* which could bestow excellence on any possible objects of comparison.[12]

At this point, we must discuss one general aspect of the philosophical problem of value which is extremely important for an understanding of the *ressentiment* delusion. It is the question of the *fundamental relation between value consciousness and desire.* There is a theory, widespread ever since Spinoza, according to which the meaning of the terms which designate positive or negative value (such as "good" or "bad") is ultimately equivalent to the statement that something is the object of desire or aversion. Good, in Spinoza's view, means "to be desired," or when there happens to be no desire at the moment, "to be capable of inciting desire." According to this theory, aspiration and aversion are therefore not founded on any preceding value consciousness. On the contrary, this value consciousness is itself nothing but the realization that we desire the object or could desire it. I have refuted these theories in detail elsewhere.[13] What interests us here is the fact that the theory is itself a product and at the same time a description of *ressentiment*. In fact, every aspiration clearly contains a value consciousness on which it is founded. It appears in the way in which we "feel" the values in question, in the act of "preferring," etc. But when we feel unable to attain certain values, *value blindness* or *value delusion* may set in. Lowering all values to the level of one's own factual desire or ability (a procedure not to be confused with the conscious act of *resignation),* construing an illusory hierarchy of values in accordance with the structure of one's personal goals and wishes — that is by no means the way in which a normal and meaningful value consciousness is realized. It is, on the contrary, the chief source of value blindness, of value delusions and illusions. The act of resignation proves that a thing can be appreciated even when it lies beyond one's reach. If the awareness of our limitations begins to limit or to dim our *value* consciousness as well — as happens, for instance, in old age with regard to the values of youth — then we have already started the movement of devaluation which will end with the defamation of the world and all its values. Only a timely act of resignation can deliver us from this tendency toward self-delusion. Only this act, moreover, keeps us from grudging others what we can no longer desire. The *independence* of our value consciousness from our wishes and abilities is further proved by the fact that perversions of the desires (such as for food or sex — for example, masochism) do not necessarily taint the sense of values. According to Ribot and others, the feelings remain normal especially in the early stages of such perversions. Thus "loathsome" food still arouses loathing, despite the impulse to eat it. Only later "the feelings gradually follow the impulse" (Ribot), but even then the sense of values may remain unaffected. There are no "perversions of value feeling" which correspond to the perversions of desire; there are only *illusions and delusions* of value feeling. This is understandable, for "feeling" or "preferring" a value is essentially an act of cognition.

Therefore a man who "slanders" the unattainable values which oppress him is by no means completely unaware of their positive character. It is not as if they simply "did not exist" in his experience. In that case we could not speak of a "delusion." Nor can we say that he feels these values, but contradicts his own experience by false judgments — that would be a case of "error" or mendacity. The phenomenal peculiarity of the *ressentiment* delusion can be described as follows: the positive values are still felt as such, but they are *overcast* by the false values and can shine through only dimly. The *ressentiment* experience is always characterized by this "transparent" presence of the true and objective values behind the illusory ones — by that obscure awareness that one lives in a *sham world* which one is unable to penetrate.[14]

As we said before, the manner in which *ressentiment* originates in individuals or groups, and the intensity it reaches, is due primarily to hereditary factors and secondarily to social structure. Let us note, however, that the social structure itself is determined by the hereditary character and the value experience of the ruling human type. Since *ressentiment* can never emerge without the mediation of a particular form of impotence, it is always one of the phenomena of "declining life." But in addition to these general preconditions, there are some *types of ressentiment* which are grounded in certain typically recurrent "situations" and whose emergence is therefore largely independent of individual temperament. It would be foolish to assert that every individual in these "situations" is necessarily gripped by *ressentiment.* I do say, however, that by virtue of their *formal character* itself — and quite apart from the character of the individuals concerned — these "situations" are *charged* with the danger of *ressentiment.*

First of all, *woman* is generally in such a situation. She is the weaker and therefore the more vindictive sex. Besides, she is always forced to compete for man's favor, and this competition centers precisely on her personal and unchangeable qualities. It is no wonder that the most vengeful deities (such as the Eumenides, that sinister generation of vipers) have mostly grown under matriarchal rule. Aeschylus' *Eumenides* present an extremely clear and plastic picture of a power which heals from *ressentiment* — that of Apollo and Athene, the deities of a new masculine civilization. We also note that the "witch" has no masculine counterpart. The strong feminine tendency to indulge in detractive gossip is further evidence; it is a form of self-cure. The danger of feminine *ressentiment* is extraordinarily intensified because both nature and custom impose upon woman a reactive and passive role in love, the domain of her most vital interest. Feelings of revenge born from rejection in the erotic sphere are always particularly subject to repression, for communication and recriminations are barred by pride and modesty. Besides, there is no tribunal which repairs such injuries, provided they violate no civil rights. It must be added that women are forced to great reserve by stronger barriers of convention and modesty. Therefore the "old maid" with her repressed cravings for tenderness, sex, and propagation, is rarely quite free of *ressentiment.* What we call "prudery," in contrast with true modesty, is but one of the numerous variants of sexual *ressentiment.* The habitual behavior of many old maids, who obsessively ferret out all sexually significant events in their surroundings in order to condemn them harshly, is nothing but sexual gratification transformed into *ressentiment* satisfaction.[15] Thus the criticism *accomplishes* the very thing it pretends to condemn. Anglo-American sexual morality is proverbially "prudish," and the reason lies in the fact that these countries have long been highly industrialized. Everything else being equal, the representative feminine groups of such countries will be increasingly recruited (probably even by hereditary selection) from those individuals who lack specifically feminine charms. Their "calculations" and their active participation and rise in an essentially utilitarian society are relatively unhampered by the cares of love and motherhood. The purer feminine type tends to be pushed into prostitution if it has no inherited fortune.[16] *Ressentiment* imitates genuine modesty by means of prudery. Conversely, it depreciates true modesty, for the prostitute's criteria come to be representative of the prevailing morality. Genuine feminine modesty, which conceals what it secretly knows to be beautiful and valuable, is interpreted as a mere "fear" of revealing physical defects or faults in dress and makeup. For the prostitute, those qualities with which she herself is insufficiently blessed are nothing but "the result of education and custom." At the end of the 18th century, especially in France, the prostitute's *ressentiment* governs not only public opinion, but actually inspires the theories of moralists and philosophers.[17]

Another situation generally exposed to *ressentiment* danger is the older generation's relation with the younger. The process of aging can only be fruitful and satisfactory if the important transitions are accompanied by free *resignation,* by the renunciation of the values

proper to the preceding stage of life. Those spiritual and intellectual
values which remain untouched by the process of aging, together with
the values of the next stage of life, must compensate for what has been
lost. Only if this happens can we cheerfully relive the values of our past
in memory, without envy for the young to whom they are still accessible. If we cannot compensate, we avoid and flee the "tormenting"
recollection of youth, thus blocking our possibilities of understanding younger people. At the same time we tend to negate the specific
values of earlier stages. No wonder that youth always has a hard fight
to sustain against the *ressentiment* of the older generation.

Yet this source of *ressentiment* is also subject to an important historical variation. In the earliest stages of civilization, old age as such is
so highly honored and respected for its experience that *ressentiment* has
hardly any chance to develop. But education spreads through print-
ing and other modern media and increasingly replaces the advantage
of experience. Younger people displace the old from their positions
and professions and push them into the defensive.[18] As the pace of
"progress" increases in all fields, and as the changes of *fashion* tend to
affect even the higher domains (such as art and science), the old can no
longer keep up with their juniors. "Novelty" becomes an ever greater
value. This is doubly true when the generation as such is seized by
an intense lust for life, and when the generations compete with each
other instead of cooperating for the creation of works which outlast
them. "Every cathedral," Werner Sombart writes, "every monastery,
every town hall, every castle of the Middle Ages bears testimony to
the transcendence of the individual's span of life: its completion spans
generations which thought that they lived for ever. Only when the
individual cut himself loose from the community which outlasted
him, did the duration of his personal life become his standard of
happiness."[19] Therefore buildings are constructed ever more hastily
— Sombart cites a number of examples. A corresponding phenomenon is the ever more rapid alternation of political regimes which goes
hand in hand with the progression of the democratic movement.[20]
But every change of government, every parliamentary change of party
domination leaves a remnant of absolute opposition against the values
of the new ruling group. This opposition is spent in *ressentiment* the
more the losing group feels unable to return to power. The "retired

official" with his followers is a typical *ressentiment* figure. Even a man like Bismarck did not entirely escape from this danger.

A further rich source of *ressentiment* lies in certain typical inter-family and intermarital relations. Above all there is the "mother-in-law," a tragic rather than ridiculous figure, especially the *son's* mother, in whose case matters are further complicated by the difference in sex. Her situation is one which the devil himself might have invented to test a hero. The child she loved since its birth and who loved her in return, the son for whom she has done everything, now turns to another woman who has done nothing for him and yet feels entitled to demand everything — and the mother is not only supposed to accept this event, but to welcome it, offer her congratulations, and receive the intruder with affection! It is truly no wonder that the songs, myths, and historical reminiscences of all nations represent the mother-in-law as an evil and insidious being. Other analogous situations are the younger children's relations with the first-born son, the older wife's with the younger husband, etc.

There is usually no *ressentiment* just where a superficial view would look for it first: in the *criminal*. The criminal is essentially an active type. Instead of repressing hatred, revenge, envy, and greed, he releases them in crime. *Ressentiment* is a basic impulse only in the crimes of spite. These are crimes which require only a minimum of action and risk and from which the criminal draws no advantage, since they are inspired by nothing but the desire to do harm. The arsonist is the purest type in point, provided that he is not motivated by the pathological urge of watching fire (a rare case) or by the wish to collect insurance. Criminals of this type strangely resemble each other. Usually they are quiet, taciturn, shy, quite settled and hostile to all alcoholic or other excesses. Their criminal act is nearly always a sudden outburst of impulses of revenge or envy which have been repressed for years. A typical cause would be the continual deflation of one's ego by the constant sight of the neighbor's rich and beautiful farm. Certain expressions of class *ressentiment,* which have lately been on the increase, also fall under this heading. I mention a crime committed near Berlin in 1912: in the darkness, the criminal stretched a wire between two trees across the road, so that the heads of passing automobilists would be shorn off. This is a typical case of *ressentiment*, for any car driver or passenger at all could be the victim, and there is no interested motive. Also in cases of slander and defamation of character, *ressentiment* often plays a major role.

Among the types of human activity which have always played a role in history, the *soldier* is least subject to *ressentiment*. Nietzsche is right in pointing out that the *priest* is most exposed to this danger, though the conclusions about religious morality which he draws from this insight are inadmissible. It is true that the very requirements of his profession, quite apart from his individual or national temperament, expose the priest more than any other human type to the creeping poison of *ressentiment*. In principle he is not supported by secular power; indeed he affirms the fundamental weakness of such power. Yet, as the representative of a concrete institution, he is to be sharply distinguished from the *homo religiosus* — he is placed in the middle of party struggle. More than any other man, he is condemned to control his emotions (revenge, wrath, hatred) at least outwardly, for he must always represent the image and principle of "peacefulness." The typical "priestly policy" of gaining victories through suffering rather than combat, or through the counterforces which the sight of the priest's suffering produces in men who believe that he unites them with God, is inspired by *ressentiment*. There is no trace of *ressentiment* in genuine martyrdom; only the false martyrdom of priestly policy is guided by it. This danger is completely avoided only when priest and *homo religiosus* coincide.[21]

In present-day society, *ressentiment* is by no means most active in the industrial proletariat (except when it is infected by the *ressentiment* of certain "leader" types), but rather in the disappearing class of artisans, in the petty bourgeoisie and among small officials. The exact causes of this phenomenon cannot be examined here.

Two specifically "spiritual" varieties of *ressentiment* humanity are the "apostate" type and to a lesser degree the "romantic" state of mind, or at least one of its essential traits.

An "apostate" is not a man who once in his life radically changes his deepest religious, political, legal, or philosophical convictions — even when this change is not continuous, but involves a sudden rupture. Even after his conversion, the true "apostate" is not primarily committed to the positive contents of his new belief and to the realization of its aims. He is motivated by the struggle against the old belief and lives only for its negation. The apostate does not affirm his new convictions for their own sake, he is engaged in a continuous chain of acts of revenge against his own spiritual past. In reality he remains a captive of this past, and the new faith is merely a handy frame of reference for negating and rejecting the old. As a religious type, the apostate is therefore at the opposite pole from the "resurrected," whose life is transformed by a new faith which is full of intrinsic meaning and value. Tertullian *(De spectaculis,* 29ff.) asserts that the sight of Roman governors burning in hell is one of the chief sources of heavenly beatitude. Nietzsche rightly cites this passage as an extreme example of apostate *ressentiment.*[22] Tertullian's sentence "credible est, quia ineptum est, certum est, quia impossibile est — credo, quia absurdum" *(De carne* ctr. 5, praeser. 7) is also a typical expression of his apostate *ressentiment.* It pungently sums up his method of defending Christianity, which is a continuous vengeance taken on the values of antiquity."[23]

To a lesser degree, a secret *ressentiment* underlies every way of thinking which attributes creative power to mere *negation* and *criticism.* Thus modern philosophy is deeply penetrated by a whole type of thinking which is nourished by *ressentiment.* I am referring to the view that the "true" and the "given" is not that which is self-evident, but rather that which is "indubitable" or "incontestable," which can be maintained against doubt and criticism. Let us also mention the principle of the "dialectical method," which wants to produce not only *non*-A, but even B through the negation of A (Spinoza: "omnis determinatio est negatio"; Hegel).[24] All the seemingly positive valuations and judgments of *ressentiment* are hidden devaluations and negations. Whenever convictions are not arrived at by direct contact with the world and the objects themselves, but indirectly through a critique of the opinions of others, the processes of thinking are impregnated with *ressentiment.* The establishment of "criteria" for testing the correctness of opinions then becomes the most important task. Genuine and fruitful criticism judges all opinions with reference to the *object itself. Ressentiment* criticism, on the contrary, accepts no "object" that has not stood the test of criticism.

In a different sense, *ressentiment* is always to some degree a determinant of the *romantic type of mind.* At least this is so when the romantic nostalgia for some past era (Hellas, the Middle Ages, etc.) is not primarily based on the values of that period, but on the wish to escape from the present. Then all praise of the "past" has the implied purpose of downgrading present-day reality. Hölderlin's love for Hellas is primary and entirely positive; it springs from deep congeniality with the Greek mind and character. On the other hand, Friedrich Schlegel's nostalgia for the Middle Ages is strongly tinged with *ressentiment.*

The formal structure of *ressentiment* expression is always the same: A is affirmed, valued, and praised not for its own intrinsic quality, but with the unverbalized intention of denying, devaluating, and denigrating B. A is "played off" against B.

I said that there is a particularly violent tension when revenge, hatred, envy, and their effects are coupled with impotence.[25] Under the impact of that tension, these affects assume the form of *ressentiment.* Not so when they are *discharged.* Therefore parliamentary institutions, even when they harm the public interest by hampering legislation and administration, are highly important as discharge mechanisms for mass and group emotions.[26] Similarly, criminal justice (which purges from revenge), the duel, and in some measure even the press — though it often spreads *ressentiment* instead of diminishing it by the public expression of opinions. If the affects are thus discharged, they are prevented from turning into that psychical dynamite which is called *ressentiment.* If the discharge is blocked, the consequence is a process which may best be designated as "repression." Nietzsche did not describe this process in detail, but he certainly had it in mind. The repressive forces are: a feeling of impotence (a pronounced awareness of inability accompanied by intense depression), fear, anxiety, and intimidation. These psychical forces become repressive especially when the steady and constant pressure of authority deprives them, as it were, of an object — i.e., when the person himself does not know "of what" he is afraid or incapable. Thus *fear,* which always has specific objects, here plays a secondary role. Much more important is that deep blockage of vital energy called "anxiety." An even better term would be "anguish" or "intimidation," to distinguish from states of anxiety with organic causes, such as respiratory trouble.[27] These forces begin by blocking only the active expression of the affects, but continue by removing them from the sphere of consciousness, so that the individual or group ceases to be clearly aware of their existence. Finally even the nascent impulse of hatred, envy, or revenge can no longer cross the threshold of consciousness.[28] At the same time, the mass of previously repressed emotions attracts and assimilates the new affect, so that each earlier repression facilitates and accelerates the continuation of the process.

We must distinguish between several components of repression. First of all, there is the repression of the original object of an emotion. I hate a certain person or want to take vengeance on him, and I am fully conscious of my reasons — of the act by which he harmed me, of the moral or physical trait which makes him distasteful to me. If I overcome my impulse by active moral energy, it does not disappear from consciousness; only its expression is checked by a clear moral judgment. But if, on the contrary, the impulse is "repressed," it becomes more and more detached from any particular reason and at length even from any particular individual. First it may come to bear on any of my enemy's qualities, activities, or judgments and on any person, relation, object, or situation which is connected with him in any way at all. The impulse "radiates" in all directions. At last it may detach itself even from the man who has injured or oppressed me. Then it turns into a negative attitude toward certain apparent traits and qualities, no matter where or in whom they are found. Here lies the origin of the well-known modern phenomenon of class hatred. Any appearance, gesture, dress, or way of speaking which is symptomatic of a "class" suffices to stir up revenge and hatred, or in other cases fear, anxiety, and respect.[29] When the repression is complete, the result is a general negativism — a sudden, violent, seemingly unsystematic and unfounded rejection of things, situations, or natural objects whose loose connection with the original cause of the hatred can only be discovered by a complicated analysis. A doctor told me about a man whom hatred has rendered incapable of reading books. Cases like this are confined to the domain of pathology. But in the stage I described, the repressed affect suddenly bursts across the threshold of consciousness whenever the repressive forces happen to relax their vigilance. It frequently finds release in unexpected inner paroxysms of invective without any specific object, and this in the midst of apparent peace of mind, during work or conversation. How often does *ressentiment* betray itself through a smile, a seemingly meaningless gesture, or a passing remark, in the midst of expressions of friendship and sympathy! When a malicious act or remark, apparently unfounded, is suddenly inserted into amicable or even loving behavior which can have lasted for months, we distinctly feel that a deeper layer of life breaks through the friendly surface. Paul suddenly recommends Christ's precept to offer the other cheek by citing Solomon's metaphor (wonderful in itself) that "coals of fire" are thus heaped on the enemy's head. Jesus' original love and humility is here made to serve a hatred which cannot content itself with revenge and seeks its satisfaction in the deeper injury of making the enemy blush with shame.[30]

But repression does not only stretch, change, and shift the original object, it also affects the *emotion itself.* Since the affect cannot outwardly express itself, it becomes active within. Detached from their original objects, the affects melt together into a venomous mass which begins to flow whenever consciousness becomes momentarily relaxed. Since all outward expression is blocked, the inner visceral sensations which accompany every affect come to prevail. All these sensations are unpleasant or even painful, so that the result is a decrease in physical well-being. The man in question no longer feels at ease in his body; it is as though he moves away from it and views it as an unpleasant object. This experience has frequently been the source of dualistic metaphysical systems — for example, in the case of the Neo-Platonists and in that of Descartes. It would be wrong to follow a well-known theory which believes that the affects are entirely composed of such visceral sensations.[31] But they do make up a substantial component of hatred, wrath, envy, revenge, etc. Yet they determine neither the particular intentionality or quality of an impulse nor the moment of its greatest intensity, but only its passive and static aspect, which varies for the different affects. In wrath it is greater than in the more "spiritual" emotions of hatred or envy. But when the visceral sensations are greatly stressed and intensified, their influence on the vital and communal instincts very often makes the affective impulses change their direction. The latter now turn against their own bearer. The result is "self-hatred," "self-torment," and "revenge against oneself."

Nietzsche wanted to explain "bad conscience" itself in this way: the "warrior" is blocked in the expression of his impulses — for example, when a small warlike nation suddenly feels included in a large and peaceful civilization — and now attacks himself. This explanation is certainly unjustified. It only accounts for a pathological form of pseudo-remorse, a false interpretation of self-directed revenge as "remorse" — a delusion which presupposes true "remorse" and a genuine "bad conscience."[32] Yet the state of affairs described by Nietzsche does exist. The example is Blaise Pascal, a man filled with *ressentiment* as few others, who succeeded with rare art in hiding the fact and in interpreting it in Christian terms: *"le moi est haïssable."* Guyau tells us that a savage who cannot commit vendetta "consumes" himself, weakens, and finally dies.[33]

Thus far about *ressentiment* itself. Now let us see what it can contribute to our understanding of certain individual and historical *moral judgments* and of entire moral systems. It goes without saying that genuine moral value judgments are never based on *ressentiment.* This criticism only applies to false judgments founded on *value delusions* and the corresponding ways of living and acting. Nietzsche is wrong in thinking that genuine morality springs from *ressentiment.* It rests on an eternal *hierarchy of values,* and its rules of preference are *fully as objective and clearly "evident"* as mathematical truths. There does exist an *ordre du coeur* and a *logique du coeur* (in Pascal's words) which the moral genius gradually uncovers in history, and it is eternal — only its apprehension and acquisition is "historical."[34] *Ressentiment* helps to subvert this eternal order in man's consciousness, to falsify its recognition, and to deflect its actualization. This should be kept in mind in the following discussion.

Basically Nietzsche says the same when he speaks of a "falsification of the value tablets" by *ressentiment.* On the other hand again, he is a skeptic and relativist in ethics. Yet "false" tablets presuppose others that are "true," or else there would be nothing but a "struggle of value systems" none of which would be "true" or "false."

*Ressentiment* can account for important developments in the history of moral judgments as well as for small everyday events. However, we must introduce an additional psychological law. We have a tendency to overcome any strong tension between desire and impotence by depreciating or denying the positive value of the desired object. At times, indeed, we go so far as to extol another object which is somehow opposed to the first. It is the old story of the fox and the sour grapes. When we have tried in vain to gain a person's love and respect, we are likely to discover in him ever new negative qualities. When we cannot obtain a thing, we comfort ourselves with the reassuring thought that it is not worth nearly as much as we believed. Initially there is only the verbalized assertion that something — a commodity, a man, or a situation — does not have the value which seemed to make us desire it. The man whose friendship we sought is not really "honest" or "brave" or "intelligent"; the grapes are not really savory; indeed they may be "sour." This is not yet a falsification of values, only a new opinion about the true qualities of the desired object. The *values* as such — intelligence, courage, honesty, the sweetness of the grapes — are acknowledged as before. The fox does not say that sweetness is bad, but that the grapes are sour. At first, such statements are only supposed to deceive the "spectators" whose mockery we fear. It is only later that their contents modify our own judgment. Yet there is a deeper motive even in the simplest cases. The negativistic statement relieves the tension between desire and impotence and reduces our depression. Our desire now seems *unmotivated;* it weakens and the tension decreases. Thus our vital energy and feeling of power rises by several degrees, though on an illusory basis. There is a tendency to modify not only our public statements, but also our own judgment. Who can fail to detect this tendency when he is told that this "inexpensive" ring or meal is much "better" than the expensive one, or to feel that it underlies the praise of "contentment," "simplicity," and "economy" in the moral sphere of the petty bourgeoisie? In this context, let us point to such sayings as "a young whore, an old saint" or "making a virtue out of necessity," and to the different evaluation of debts by merchants or nobles.

This law of the release of tension through illusory valuation gains new significance, full of infinite consequences, for the *ressentiment* attitude. To its very core, the mind of *ressentiment* man is filled with envy, the impulse to detract, malice, and secret vindictiveness. These affects have become fixed attitudes, detached from all determinate objects. Independently of his will, this man's attention will be instinctively drawn by all events which can set these affects in motion. The *ressentiment* attitude even plays a role in the formation of perceptions, expectations, and memories. It automatically selects those aspects of experience which can justify the factual application of this pattern of feeling. Therefore such phenomena as joy, splendor, power, happiness, fortune, and strength magically attract the man of *ressentiment.* He cannot pass by, he has to look at them, whether he "wants" to or not. But at the same time he wants to avert his eyes, for he is tormented by the craving to possess them and knows that his desire is vain. The first result of this inner process is a characteristic *falsification* of the *world view.* Regardless of what he observes, his world has a peculiar structure of emotional stress. The more the impulse to turn away from those positive values prevails, the more he turns without transition to their negative opposites, on which he concentrates increasingly. He has an urge to scold, to depreciate, to belittle whatever he can. Thus he involuntarily "slanders" life and the world in order to justify his inner pattern of value experience.

But this instinctive falsification of the world view is only of limited effectiveness. Again and again the *ressentiment* man encounters happiness, power, beauty, wit, goodness, and other phenomena of positive life. They exist and impose themselves, however much he may shake his fist against them and try to explain them away. He cannot escape the tormenting conflict between desire and impotence. Averting his eyes is sometimes impossible and in the long run ineffective. When such a quality irresistibly forces itself upon his attention, the very sight suffices to produce an impulse of hatred against its bearer, who has never harmed or insulted him. Dwarfs and cripples, who already feel humiliated by the outward appearance of the others, often show this peculiar hatred — this hyena-like and ever-ready ferocity. Precisely because this kind of hostility is not caused by the "enemy's" actions and behavior, it is deeper and more irreconcilable than any other. It is not directed against transitory attributes, but against the other person's very essence and being. Goethe has this type of "enemy" in mind when he writes: "Why complain about enemies? — Could those become your friends — To whom your very existence — Is an eternal silent reproach?" (*West-Eastern Divan*). The very existence of this "being," His mere appearance, becomes a silent, unadmitted "reproach." Other disputes can be settled, but not this! Goethe knew, for his rich and great existence was the ideal target of *ressentiment*. His very appearance was bound to make the poison flow.[35]

But even this apparently unfounded hatred is not yet the most characteristic achievement of *ressentiment*. Even here, it is still directed against particular persons or (as in class hatred) particular groups. Its effect is much more profound when it goes beyond such determinate hostilities — when it does not lead to a falsification of the world view, but perverts the *sense of values* itself. What Nietzsche calls "falsification of the tablets of value" is built on this foundation. In this new phase, the man of *ressentiment* no longer turns away from the positive values, nor does he wish to destroy the men and things endowed with them. Now the values themselves are inverted: those values which are positive to any normal feeling become negative. The man of *ressentiment* cannot justify or even understand his own existence and sense of life in terms of positive values such as power, health, beauty, freedom, and independence. Weakness, fear, anxiety, and a slavish disposition prevent him from obtaining them. Therefore he comes to feel that "all this is vain anyway" and that salvation lies in the opposite phenomena: poverty, suffering, illness, and death. This "sublime revenge" of *ressentiment* (in Nietzsche's words) has indeed played a creative role in the history of value systems. It is "sublime," for the impulses of revenge against those who are strong, healthy, rich, or handsome now disappear entirely. *Ressentiment* has brought deliverance from the inner torment of these affects. Once the sense of values has shifted and the new judgments have spread, such people cease to be enviable, hateful, and worthy of revenge. They are unfortunate and to be pitied, for they are beset with "evils." Their sight now awakens feelings of gentleness, pity, and commiseration. When the reversal of values comes to dominate accepted morality and is invested with the power of the ruling ethos, it is transmitted by tradition, suggestion, and education to those who are endowed with the seemingly devaluated qualities. They are struck with a "bad conscience" and secretly condemn themselves. The "slaves," as Nietzsche says, infect the "masters." *Ressentiment* man, on the other hand, now feels "good," "pure," and "human" — at least in the conscious layers of his mind. He is delivered from hatred, from the tormenting desire of an impossible revenge, though deep down his poisoned sense of life and the true values may still shine through the illusory ones. There is no more calumny, no more defamation of particular persons or things. The systematic perversion and reinterpretation of the values *themselves* is much more effective than the "slandering" of persons or the falsification of the world view could ever be.

What is called "falsification of the value tablets," "reinterpretation," or "transvaluation" should not be mistaken for conscious lying. Indeed, it goes beyond the sphere of judging. It is not that the positive value is felt as such and that it is merely declared to be "bad." Beyond all conscious lying and falsifying, there is a deeper "organic mendacity." Here the falsification is not formed in consciousness, but at the same stage of the mental process as the impressions and value feelings themselves: *on the road* of experience into consciousness. There is "organic mendacity" whenever a man's mind admits only those impressions which serve his "interest" or his instinctive attitude. Already in the process of mental reproduction and recollection, the contents of his experience are modified in this direction. He who is "mendacious" has no need to lie! In his case, the automatic process of forming recollections, impressions, and feelings is involuntarily slanted, so that conscious falsification becomes unnecessary. Indeed the most honest and upright convictions may prevail in the periphery of consciousness. The apprehension of values follows this pattern, to the point of their complete reversal. The *value judgment* is based on this original "falsification." It is itself entirely "true," "genuine," and "honest," for the value it affirms is really felt to be positive.[36]

# *Ressentiment* AND
# MORAL VALUE JUDGMENT

The recognition that there have been *several* "moralities" in the world, not just one, is one of the most important results of modern ethics.[1] One tends to think that this is old news, as old as the insight into the so-called "historical relativity" of customs. That is a complete error. The adherents of so-called ethical relativism — for example, the modern positivists Comte, Mill, Spencer, et al. — are precisely those who have most thoroughly misunderstood the whole question. The relativists merely show that different ways of acting have been deemed useful for "human welfare," the "exaltation of life," or whatever else the relativist philosopher himself judges to be the greatest good — and that these differences depend upon the level of knowledge and civilization. Thus in a preponderantly military society, where war is a means of acquisition, such virtues as courage and bravery are more useful for the "general welfare" than industry, diligence, and honesty, which will find preference in an industrial society. Often, as among the early Germanic tribes, pillage is a smaller crime than theft. But the relativists affirm that the basic *value* has remained the same. All variations are due to the different historical circumstances to which this basic value (for example, welfare) is applied. But a transformation of values is quite another thing. When we say that there have been several moralities, we mean that *the rules of preference between the values themselves* have varied, quite apart from all changes in the external conditions of life. A "morality" is a system of preference between the values themselves, a "moral constitution" which must be discovered *behind* the concrete valuations of a nation and an era. This system itself can undergo an evolution which has nothing at all to do with the growing adaptation of actions and judgments to changing conditions. In the latter case, the evaluations of certain actions, convictions, or types of men may have changed, but the ultimate criterion (such as general welfare) has remained the same. But there have been primary transformations of the moral systems themselves, independently of mere adaptations. Actually, the so-called ethical "relativists" have always been the absolutists of their own particular periods. They interpret the variations in moral judgments as stages in the "development" toward present-day morality, by which they wrongly measure the past. They do not even see the primary variations in the ways of judging, the rules of preference themselves. It is ethical absolutism, the doctrine which teaches that there are eternal evident laws of preference and a corresponding eternal hierarchy of values, which has recognized and could afford to acknowledge this much more far-reaching relativity of value judgments. The relation between the various moralities and that eternally valid ethics is approximately the same as that between the different astronomical systems (for example, the Ptolemaic and the Copernican system) and the ideal system sought by astronomy. That intrinsically valid system is represented more or less adequately in the different moralities. The realities of life are themselves co-determined by the dominant moralities. Their emergence is influenced by primary judgments and decisions whose variations cannot in turn be explained as adaptations to these moralities.[2] The history of moralities should learn from a recent insight of art history: the modifications of the ideal of artistic representation and the stylistic forms are not exclusively determined by the changes in material means and technical know-how (as for example Semper thought), but the "artistic intention" itself has been subject to great change.[3] Thus if the Greeks had no technical civilization, it is not because they were incapable (or "as yet" incapable) of creating one, but because they did not *wish* to create it. It would have run counter to the spirit of their "morality." By "morality" we mean the rules of preference *themselves* which govern a nation and an era, not the philosophical and scientific "representation" or "systematization" of these rules, which merely *deals* with a "morality."

*Ressentiment* brings about its most important achievement when it determines a whole "morality," perverting the rules of preference until what was "evil" appears to be "good." If we look at European history, we are struck by the enormous effectiveness of *ressentiment* in the formation of moralities. Our task is to determine its role in the formation of *Christian morality* on one hand, of *modern bourgeois morality* on the other. Here our view sharply departs from that of Friedrich Nietzsche:

We believe that the Christian values can very easily be perverted into *ressentiment* values and have often been thus conceived. But *the core of Christian ethics has not grown on the soil of ressentiment.* On the other hand, we believe that *the core of bourgeois morality,* which gradually replaced Christian morality ever since the 13th century and culminated in the French Revolution, *is rooted in ressentiment.* In the modern social movement, *ressentiment* has become an important determinant and has increasingly modified established morality.

First let us examine whether Christian morality was nourished and sustained by *ressentiment.*

## CHRISTIAN MORALITY AND *Ressentiment*

Friedrich Nietzsche characterizes the idea of Christian love as the most delicate flower of *ressentiment.* He believes that through this idea the *ressentiment* accumulated by an oppressed and at the same time vindictive nation, whose God was the "God of revenge" even when it was still politically and socially independent, is justified before this nation's consciousness.[1]

If we fully appreciate the revolutionary character of the change which leads from tire ancient to the Christian idea of love — Nietzsche himself has done this only vaguely and inexactly — this Nietzschean statement is much less paradoxical than would appear at first sight. Indeed, his discovery is one of the most profound which has ever been made on this question and is fully worthy of the most serious consideration. I stress this all the more because I consider his theory to be *completely mistaken.*

The Greek and Roman philosophers and poets have expressed the significance and value of love in ancient morality with admirable clarity. A brief summary, without reference to specific sources, will be sufficient here. First of all, logical form, law, justice — in short, the element of measure and equality in the distribution of goods and evils — are superior to love. Even though Plato, in the *Symposium* for example, establishes great differences in value between the various kinds of love, in Greek eyes the whole phenomenon of "love" belongs to the domain of the senses. It is a form of "desire," of "need," etc., which is foreign to the most perfect kind of being. This view is the natural corollary of the extremely questionable ancient division of human nature into "reason" and "sensuality," into a part that is formative and one that is formed. In the sphere of Christian morality, on the other hand, love is explicitly placed above the rational domain — love "that makes more blessed than all reason" (Augustine). This comes out quite clearly in the parable of the prodigal son.[2] *"Agape"* and *"caritas"* are sharply and dualistically separated from *"eros"* and *"amor,"* whereas the Greeks and Romans — though they do acknowledge distinctions in value — rather see a continuity between these types of love. Christian love is a spiritual intentionality which transcends the natural sphere, defeating and superseding the psychological mechanism of the natural instincts (such as hatred against one's enemies, revenge, and desire for retaliation). It can place a man in a completely new state of life. But that is not essential here. The most important difference between the ancient and Christian views of love lies in the *direction of its movement.* All ancient philosophers, poets, and moralists agree that love is a striving, an aspiration of the "lower" toward the "higher," the "unformed" toward the "formed," the "μὴ ὄν" towards the "ὄν," "appearance" towards "essence," "ignorance" towards "knowledge," a "mean between fullness and privation," as Plato says in the *Symposium.* Thus in all human love relations, such as marriage or friendship, a distinction must be made between a "lover" and a "beloved," and the latter is always nobler and more perfect. He is the *model* for the lover's being, willing, and acting.[3] This conception, which grew from the relations of life in antiquity, finds its clearest expression in the numerous forms of Greek metaphysics. Already Plato says: "We would not love if we were Gods." For the most perfect form of being cannot know "aspiration" or "need."[4] Here love is only a road to something else, a *"methodos."* And according to Aristotle, in all things there is rooted an upward urge (ὀρέγεσθαι and ἐφίεσθαι) towards the deity, the Noῦς, the self-sufficient thinker who "moves" the world as "prime mover." He does not move it as a being whose will and activity is directed toward the outside, but "as the beloved moves the lover" (Aristotle) — as it were *attracting,* enticing, and tempting it. In this idea, with its unique sublimity, beauty, and ancient coolness, the essence of the ancient conception of love is raised into the absolute and boundless. The universe is a great chain of dynamic spiritual entities, of forms of being ranging from the "prima materia" up to man — a chain in which the lower always strives for and is attracted by the higher, which never turns back but aspires upward in its turn. This process continues up to the deity, which itself does not love, but represents the eternally unmoving and unifying *goal* of all these aspirations of love. Too little attention has been given to the peculiar relation between this idea of love and the principle of the "agon," the ambitious contest for the goal, which dominated Greek life in all its aspects — from the Gymnasium and the games to dialectics and the political life of the Greek city states. Even the objects try to surpass each other in a race for victory, in a cosmic "agon" for the deity. Here the prize that will crown the victor is extreme: it is a participation in the essence, knowledge, and abundance of "being." Love is only the dynamic principle, immanent in the universe, which sets in motion this great "agon" of all things for the deity.

Let us compare this with the Christian conception. In that conception there takes place what might be called a *reversal in the movement of love.* The Christian view boldly denies the Greek axiom that love is an aspiration of the lower towards the higher. On the contrary, now the criterion of love is that the nobler stoops to the vulgar, the healthy to the sick, the rich to the poor, the handsome to the ugly, the good and saintly to the bad and common, the Messiah to the sinners and publicans. The Christian is not afraid, like the ancient, that he might lose something by doing so, that he might impair his own nobility. He acts in the peculiarly pious conviction that through this "condescension," through this self-abasement and "self-renunciation" he gains the highest good and becomes equal to God.[5] The change in the notion of God and his fundamental relation to man and the world is not the cause, but the *consequence* of this reversal in the movement of love. God is no longer the eternal unmoving goal — like a star — for the love of all things, moving the world as "the beloved moves the lover." Now the very *essence* of God is to love and serve. Creating, willing, and acting are derived from these original qualities. The eternal "first mover" of the world is replaced by the "creator" who created it "out of love."[6] An event that is monstrous for the man of antiquity, that is absolutely paradoxical according to his axioms, is supposed to have taken place in Galilee: God spontaneously "descended" to man, became a servant, and died the bad servant's death on the cross! Now the precept of loving good and hating evil, loving one's friend and hating one's enemy, becomes meaningless. There is no longer any "highest good" independent of and beyond the act and movement of love! Love itself is the highest of all goods! The *summum bonum* is no longer the value of a thing, but of an act, the value of love itself *as love* — not for its results and achievements. Indeed, the achievements of love are only symbols and proofs of its *presence in the person.* And thus God himself becomes a "person" who has no "idea of the good," no "form and order," no Λόγος above him, but only below him — through his deed of love. He becomes a God who loves — for the man of antiquity something like a square circle, an "imperfect perfection." How strongly did Neo-Platonic criticism stress that love is a form of "need" and "aspiration" which indicates "imperfection," and that it is false, presumptuous, and sinful to attribute it to the deity! But there is another great innovation: in the Christian view, love is a non-sensuous act of the *spirit* (not a mere state of feeling, as for the moderns), but it is nevertheless not a striving and desiring, and even less a need.[7] These acts consume themselves in the realization of the desired goal. Love, however, *grows* in its action. And there are no longer any rational principles, any rules or justice, higher than love, independent of it and preceding it, which should guide its action and its distribution among men according to their value. All are worthy of love — friends and enemies, the good and the evil, the noble and the common.[8] Whenever I see badness in another, I must feel partly guilty, for I must say to myself: "Would that man be bad if you had loved him enough?"[9] In the Christian view, *sensuous* sympathy — together with its root in our most powerful impulse — is not the source, but the partial *blockage* of love.[10] Therefore not only positive wrongdoing, but even the failure to love is "guilt." Indeed, it is *the* guilt at the bottom of all guiltiness.

Thus the picture has shifted immensely. This is no longer a band of men and things that surpass each other in striving up to the deity. It is a band in which every member looks back toward those who are further removed from God and comes to resemble the deity by helping and serving them — for this great urge to love, to serve, to bend down, is God's own essence.

I do not here analyze the constructive forms which this emotional reversal has taken in dogma, theology, and religious worship, though the task is tempting — especially in the cases of Paul and Augustine. Confining myself to the essential, I ask: whence this reversal? Is *ressentiment* really its mainspring?

The more I reflected on this question, the more clearly I realized that the root of Christian love is entirely *free* of *ressentiment,* but that *ressentiment* can very easily use it for its own purposes by simulating an emotion which corresponds to this idea. This simulation is often so perfect that even the sharpest observer can no longer distinguish real love from *ressentiment* which poses as love.[11]

There are two fundamentally different ways for the strong to bend down to the weak, for the rich to help the poor, for the more perfect life to help the "less perfect." This action can be motivated by a powerful feeling of security, strength, and inner salvation, of the invincible fullness of one's own life and existence. All this unites into the clear awareness that one is *rich enough* to share one's being and possessions. Love, sacrifice, help, the descent to the small and the weak, here spring from a spontaneous overflow of force, accompanied by bliss and deep inner calm. Compared to this natural readiness for love and sacrifice, all specific "egoism," the concern for oneself and one's interest, and even the instinct of "self-preservation" are signs of a blocked and weakened life. Life is essentially expansion, development, growth in plenitude, and not "self-preservation," as a false doctrine has it. Development, expansion, and growth are not epiphenomena of mere preservative forces and cannot be reduced to the preservation of the "better adapted." We do believe that life itself can be sacrificed for values higher than life, but this does not mean that all sacrifice runs counter to life and its advancement.[12] There is a form of sacrifice which is a free renunciation of one's own vital abundance, a beautiful and natural overflow of one's forces. Every living being has a natural instinct of sympathy for other living beings, which increases with their proximity and similarity to himself. Thus we sacrifice ourselves for beings with whom we feel united and solidary, in contrast to everything "dead." This sacrificial impulse is by no means a later acquisition of life, derived from originally egoistic urges. It is an *original* component of life and *precedes* all those particular "aims" and "goals" which calculation, intelligence, and reflection impose upon it later. *We have an urge to sacrifice* before we ever know why, for what, and for whom!

Jesus' view of nature and life, which sometimes shines through his speeches and parables in fragments and hidden allusions, shows quite clearly that he understood this fact. When he tells us not to worry about eating and drinking, it is not because he is indifferent to life and its preservation, but because he sees also a *vital* weakness in all "worrying" about the next day, in all concentration on one's own physical well-being. The ravens with neither storehouse nor barn, the lilies which do not toil and spin and which God still arrays more gloriously than Solomon (Luke 12:24 and 27) — they are symbols of that profound total impression he has of life: all voluntary concentration on one's own bodily well-being, all worry and anxiety, hampers rather than furthers the creative force which instinctively and beneficently governs all life. "And which of you with taking thought can add to his stature one cubit?" (Luke 12:25). This kind of indifference to the external *means* of life (food, clothing, etc.) is not a sign of indifference to life and its value, but rather of a profound and secret confidence in life's own *vigor* and of an inner security from the mechanical accidents which may befall it. A gay, light, bold, knightly indifference to external circumstances, drawn from the depth of life itself — that is the feeling which inspires these words! Egoism and fear of death are signs of a declining, sick, and broken life. Let us remember that the fear of death was so widespread in antiquity that some schools of philosophy, that of the Epicureans among others, see the aim of philosophy in freeing man from it.[13] The periods of greatest vitality were indifferent to life and its end. Such indifference is itself a state of mind which has vital value.

*This* kind of love and sacrifice for the weaker, the sick, and the small springs from inner security and vital plenitude. In addition to this vital security, there is that other feeling of bliss and security, that awareness of safety in the fortress of ultimate being itself (Jesus calls it "kingdom of God"). The deeper and more central it is, the more man *can* and *may* be almost playfully "indifferent" to his "fate" in the peripheral zones of his existence — indifferent to whatever is still accessible to "happiness" and "suffering," "pleasure" and "displeasure," "joy" and "pain."[14]

When a person's spontaneous impulse of love and sacrifice finds a specific goal, an opportunity for applying itself, he does not welcome it as a chance to plunge into such phenomena as poverty, sickness, or ugliness. He does not help this struggling life because of those negative values, but *despite* them — he helps in order to develop whatever may still be sound and positive. He does not love such life *because* it is sick, poor, small, and ugly, and he does not passively dwell upon these attributes. The positive vital values (and even more, of course, the spiritual personal values of that individual) are completely *independent* of these defects and lie much deeper. Therefore his own fullness of life can (and therefore "should") overcome his natural reaction of fearing and fleeing them, and his love should helpfully develop whatever is positive in the poor or sick man. He does not love sickness and poverty, but what is *behind* them, and his help is directed *against* these evils. When Francis of Assisi kisses festering wounds and does not even kill the bugs that bite him, but leaves his body to them as a hospitable home, these acts (if seen from the outside) could be signs of perverted instincts and of a perverted valuation. But that is not actually the case. It is not a lack of nausea or a delight in the pus which makes St. Francis act in this way. He has overcome his nausea through a deeper feeling of life and vigor! This attitude is completely different from that of recent modern realism in art and literature, the exposure of social misery, the description of little people, the wallowing in the morbid — a typical *ressentiment* phenomenon. Those people saw something bug-like in everything that lives, whereas Francis sees the holiness of "life" even in bug.[15]

In the ancient notion of love, on the other hand, there is an element of *anxiety.* The noble fears the descent to the less noble, is afraid of being infected and pulled down. The "sage" of antiquity does not have the same firmness, the same inner certainty of himself and his own value, as the genius and hero of Christian love.

A further characteristic: Love in Jesus' sense helps energetically. But it *does not consist* in the desire to help, or even in "benevolence." Such love is, as it were, immersed in positive value, and helping and benevolence are only its consequences. The fake love of *ressentiment* man offers no real help, since for his perverted sense of values, evils like "sickness" and "poverty" have become goods. He believes, after all, that "God giveth grace to the humble" (I Peter, 5:5), so that raising the small or curing the sick would mean *removing* them from their salvation.[16]

But this does not mean that the value of love in the genuine Christian sense lies in the usefulness of its helping deed. The usefulness may be great with little love or none at all, and it may be small while love is great. The widow's mites (Mark 12:42-24) are more to God than the gifts of the rich — not because they are only "mites" or because the giver is only a "poor widow," but because her action reveals *more love*. Thus the increase in value originally always lies on the side of him who loves, *not* on the side of him who is helped. Love is no spiritual "institution of charity" and is not in contrast to one's own bliss. In the very act of self-renunciation, the person eternally wins himself. He is blissful in loving and giving, for "it is more blessed to give than to receive" (Acts 20:35). Love is not valuable and does not bestow distinction on the lover because it is just one of the countless forces which further human or social welfare. No, the value is love *itself*, its penetration of the whole person — the higher, firmer, and richer life and existence of which its movement is the sign and the gem. The important thing is not the amount of welfare, it is that there should be a *maximum of love* among men. The act of helping is the direct and adequate *expression* of love, not its meaning or "purpose." Its meaning lies in itself, in its illumination of the soul, in the nobility of the loving soul in the act of love. Therefore nothing can be further removed from this genuine concept of Christian love than all kinds of "socialism," "social feeling," "altruism," and other subaltern modern things. When the rich youth is told to divest himself of his riches and give them to the poor, it is really not in order to help the "poor" and to effect a better distribution of property in the interest of general welfare. Nor is it because poverty as such is supposed to be better than wealth. The order is given because the *act* of giving away, and the spiritual freedom and abundance of love which manifest themselves in this act, ennoble the youth and make him even "richer" than he is.

This element is also present in the metaphysico-religious conceptions of man's relation to God. The old covenant between God and man, which is the root of all "legality," is replaced by the love between God and his children. And even the love "for God" is not to be founded on his works alone, in gratitude for his constant gifts, his care and maintenance. All these experiences of God's actions and works are only means to make us look up to "eternal love" and to the infinite abundance of value of which these works are but the proof. They should be admired and loved only because they are works of love! This conception was still very strong among the best medieval Christians. Thus Hugo de Saint Victor, in his *Soliloquy on the Earnest Money of the Soul (Soliloquium de arrha animae),* refers to a love which is founded only on God's works and good deeds as "a love like a whore"! But already in Solomon's proverb "When I have you, I do not ask for heaven or earth" we find this strict opposition to the idea of the covenant — an idea which contains the germs of that love based on gratitude which typifies all average religiosity. We should not love God because of his heaven and earth: we should love heaven and earth because they are God's, and because they adumbrate eternal love by means of sensible *expression* rather than as a purposive idea.[17] The same is true for the concept of God. Antiquity believed that the forces of love in the universe were limited. Therefore they were to be used sparingly, and everyone was to be loved only according to his value. The idea that love has its origin in God himself, the infinite Being, that he himself is infinite love and mercy, naturally entails the precept of loving both the good and the bad, the just and the sinners, one's friends and one's enemies. Genuine love, transcending the natural sphere, is manifested most clearly when we love our enemy. The ancient precept of loving the good and the just, and of hating the evil and the unjust, is now rejected as "pharisaism." Indeed, in a wider metaphysical context, God is not only the "creator" (instead of a mere ideal, a perfect being, the goal of the world's upward movement), but even the "creator out of love." His creation, the "world" itself, is nothing but the momentary coagulation of an infinitely flowing gesture of love. The deity of Greek metaphysics is the ideal of the "sage" in its absolute form: a logical egoist, a being closed in itself, self-observing and self-thinking ($\nu\acute{o}\eta\sigma\iota\varsigma$ $\nu o\acute{\eta}\sigma\epsilon\omega\varsigma$), who cares little about the course of earthly events and is not truly responsible for the world.[18] The Christian deity is a *personal* God who created the "world" out of an infinite overflow of love — not because he wanted to help anyone or anything, for "nothing" existed before, but only to express his superabundance of love. This new notion of the deity is the conceptual theological expression of the changed attitude toward life.

There is not a trace of *ressentiment* in all this. Nothing but a blissful ability to stoop, born from an abundance of force and nobility!

But there is a completely different way of stooping to the small, the lowly, and the common, even though it may seem almost the same. Here love does not spring from an abundance of vital power, from firmness and security. Here it is only a euphemism for *escape,* for the inability to "remain at home" with oneself *(chez soi).* Turning toward others is but the secondary consequence of this urge to flee from oneself. One cannot love anybody without turning away from oneself. However, the crucial question is whether this movement is prompted by the desire to turn toward a positive value, or whether the intention is a radical escape from oneself. "Love" of the second variety is inspired by self-hatred, by hatred of one's own weakness and misery. The mind is always on the point of departing for distant places. Afraid of seeing itself and its inferiority, it is driven to give itself to the other — not because of his worth, but merely for the sake of his "otherness." Modern philosophical jargon has found a revealing term for this phenomenon, one of the many modern substitutes for love: "altruism." This love is not directed at a previously discovered positive value, nor does any such value flash up in the act of loving: there is nothing but the urge to turn away from oneself and to lose oneself in other people's business. We all know a certain type of man frequently found among socialists, suffragettes, and all people with an ever-ready "social conscience" — the kind of person whose social activity is quite clearly prompted by inability to keep his attention focused on himself, on his own tasks and problems.[19] Looking away from oneself is here mistaken for love! Isn't it abundantly clear that "altruism," the interest in "others" and their lives, has nothing at all to do with love? The malicious or envious person also forgets his own interest, even his "preservation." He only thinks about the other man's feelings, about the harm and the suffering he inflicts on him.[20] Conversely, there is a form of genuine "self-love" which has nothing at all to do with "egoism."[21] It is precisely the essential feature of egoism that it does not apprehend the full value of the isolated self. The egoist sees himself only with regard to the others, as a member of society who wishes to possess and acquire *more* than the others.[22] Self-directedness or other-directedness have no essential bearing on the specific quality of love or hatred. These acts are different *in themselves,* quite independently of their direction.

Thus the "altruistic" urge is really a form of hatred, of self-hatred, *posing* as its opposite ("Love") in the false perspective of consciousness. In the same way, in *ressentiment* morality, love for the "small," the "poor," the "weak," and the "oppressed" is really disguised hatred, repressed envy, an impulse to detract, etc., directed against the opposite phenomena: "wealth," "strength," "power," "*largesse.*" When hatred does not dare to come out into the open, it can be easily expressed in the form of ostensible love — love for something which has features that are the opposite of those of the hated object. This can happen in such a way that the hatred remains secret. When we hear that falsely pious, unctuous tone (it is the tone of a certain "socially-minded" type of priest), sermonizing that love for the "small" is our first duty, love for the "humble" in spirit, since God gives "grace" to them, then it is often only hatred posing as Christian love. We clearly feel how the sight of these phenomena fills the mind with secret "satisfaction" and how they themselves are loved, not the higher values which may lie behind them. Nor can the helping deed be the important thing in this perspective, since it would make the "small" less agreeable to God and would therefore be an expression of hatred. The whole value lies in dwelling upon these phenomena. And when we are told, in the same tone, that these people will be rewarded in "heaven" for their distress, and that "heaven" is the exact reverse of the earthly order ("the first shall be last"), we distinctly feel how the *ressentiment*-laden man transfers to God the vengeance he himself cannot wreak on the great. In this way, he can satisfy his revenge at least in imagination, with the aid of an other-worldly mechanism of rewards and punishments. The core of the *ressentiment* Christian's idea of God is still the avenging Jehovah. The only difference is that revenge is now masked as sham love for the "small." There is no longer any organic and experienced bond between the "kingdom of God" and the visible realm, so that the values and laws of retaliation of the former have ceased to be simply a purer and more perfect expression of those which already appear in life. The "kingdom of God" has become the "other world," which stands mechanically beside "this world" — an opposition unknown to the strongest periods of Christianity. It is merely a plane of being where the shadows of the people and events we experienced carry on a dance led by *ressentiment,* according to a rhythm which is simply opposite to that of the earth.

It is true that Jesus is mainly interested in the poor, the sick, the wretched and oppressed, the publicans, and shows a mysteriously strange affection for the sinners (cf. the "adulteress," the sinful woman anointing Jesus, the parable of the "prodigal son"). He cannot refer to the "good and the just" without some irony. Statements like "They that are whole, have no need of the physician, but they that are sick: I came not to call the righteous, but sinners to repentance" (Mark 2:17) do not explain these tendencies — let us remember that he rejects the epithet "good" even for himself ("Why callest thou me good? None is good save one, *that* is God." Luke 18:19). Yet all this cannot make me believe in *ressentiment* on his part. His statements, so it seems to me, do not mean that salvation is dependent on those negative qualities, as *ressentiment* would have it. Their true meaning lies in the paradoxical form in which the highest and ultimate *personality values* are declared to be *independent* of contrasts like rich and poor, healthy and sick, etc. The world had become accustomed to considering the social hierarchy, based on status, wealth, vital strength, and power, as an exact image of the ultimate values of morality and personality. The only way to disclose the discovery of a new and higher *sphere* of being and life, of the "kingdom of God" whose order is independent of that worldly and vital hierarchy, was to stress the vanity of the old values in this higher order. There are only certain passages, chiefly in the Gospel of Luke, which may go beyond this interpretation, for they seem to represent the kingdom of God as the reverse of the earthly realm. Thus the Beatitudes in Luke 6:20-22, 24-26: "Blessed be ye poor: for yours is the kingdom of God. Blessed are ye that hunger now: for ye shall be filled. Blessed are ye that weep now, for ye shall laugh. Blessed are ye when men shall hate you, and when they shall separate you *from their company,* and shall reproach you, and cast out your name as evil, for the Son of man's sake ...." And further: "But woe unto you that are rich: for ye have received your consolation. Woe unto you that are full: for ye shall hunger. Woe unto you that laugh now: for ye shall mourn and weep. Woe unto you when all men shall speak well of you: for so did their fathers to the false Prophets."

Another example is the blunt assertion (in Luke 18:25) that "it is easier for a camel to go through a needle's eye, than for a rich man to enter into the kingdom of God," though it is considerably softened by the preceding passage: "How hardly shall they that have riches, enter into the kingdom of God" — and also by the subsequent statement that God can lead even the rich into the kingdom of God. Here indeed it seems to me that the author's form of presentation cannot be absolved of *ressentiment.* Yet this trend is confined to Luke, and even there it is a personal coloring in the *presentation* of ideas which are by no means rooted in *ressentiment.*

Even the precepts "Love your enemies, do good to them which hate you, bless them that curse you, and pray for them which despitefully use you. And unto him that smiteth thee on the one cheek, offer also the other: and him that taketh away thy cloak, forbid not to take thy coat also" (Luke 6:27-29) do not demand a passivity which is only "justified" by the inability to seek revenge (as Nietzsche wrongly thought). Nor do they seek to shame the enemy in secret vengefulness, or indicate a hidden self-torment which satisfies itself through paradoxical behavior. These precepts demand an extreme activity against the natural instincts which push us in the opposite direction. They are born from the Gospel's profound spirit of individualism, which refuses to let one's own actions and conduct depend in any way on somebody else's acts. The Christian refuses to let his acts be mere *reactions* — such conduct would lower him to the level of his enemy. The act is to grow organically from the person, "as the fruit from the tree." "A good man out of the good treasure of his heart, bringeth forth good things: and an evil man out of the evil treasure, bringeth forth evil things." "For out of the abundance of the heart the mouth speaketh." (Matthew 12:34 and 35). What the Gospel demands is not a reaction which is the reverse of the natural reaction, as if it said: "Because he strikes you on the cheek, tend the other" — but a rejection of all reactive activity, of any participation in common and average ways of acting and standards of judgment.

I spoke of Jesus' "mysterious" affection for the sinners, which is closely related to his ever-ready militancy against the scribes and pharisees, against every kind of social respectability. Is this an element of *ressentiment?* Certainly this attitude contains a kind of awareness that the great transformation of life, the radical change in outlook he demands of man (in Christian parlance it is called "rebirth") is more accessible to the sinner than to the "just," who tries to approach the ideal of the law step by step and day by day. In the "sinner" there is the powerful movement of life and, as it were, the great possibility! We must add that Jesus is deeply skeptical toward all those who can feign the good man's blissful existence through the simple lack of strong instincts and vitality. But all this does not suffice to explain this mysterious affection. In it there is something which can scarcely be expressed and must be felt. When the noblest men are in the company of the "good" — even of the truly "good," not only of the pharisees — they are often overcome by a sudden impetuous yearning to go to the sinners, to suffer and struggle at their side and to share their grievous, gloomy lives. This is truly no temptation by the pleasures of sin, nor a demoniacal love for its "sweetness," nor the attraction of the forbidden or the lure of novel experiences. It is an outburst of tempestuous love and tempestuous compassion for *all* men who are felt as one, indeed for the universe as a whole; a love which makes it seem frightful that only some should be "good," while the others are "bad" and reprobate. In such moments, love and a deep *sense of solidarity* are repelled by the thought that we alone should be "good," together with some others. This fills us with a kind of loathing for those who can accept this privilege, and we have an urge to move away from them.

Expressed in sober concepts, this is only a consequence of the new Christian idea that the act of love as such is the *summum bonum,* as "abundant love" (Luther), independent of the value of its object. In the view of the ancients, love for the bad is bad itself, while here the value of the *act* of loving stands out even more distinctly when the sinner is its object.

Another element must be added. The notorious "sinner" is also one who *acknowledges* the evil in his soul. I am not only thinking of verbal confession, as before a tribunal, but also of admission before oneself or through the deed in which the sinful desire has issued. Let what he acknowledges be evil and sinful: the fact *that* he does it is not evil; it is good! In this way he purges his soul and prevents the spreading of the poison. But if he represses his evil impulses, the poison will

penetrate more and more deeply, and at the same time it will become
ever more hidden from his knowledge and conscience. Finally even
the "beam in one's own eye" will no longer be felt — but the "mote
in one's brother's eye" all the more! Therefore the sinful deed which
is followed by remorse — and does not remorse begin with the very
deed insofar as it is a confession? — is better in Jesus' eyes than the
repression of the sinful impulse and the consequent poisoning of a
man's inner core, which can easily go with the conviction of being
good and just before the law. That is why "joy shall be in heaven over
one sinner that repenteth, more than over ninety and nine just persons" (Luke 15:7). That is why we read: "To whom little is forgiven,
the same loveth little" (Luke 7:47). Jesus, who in his Sermon on the
Mount sees adultery in the very act of "looking on a woman to lust after
her" (Matt. 5:28), must judge like this to be consistent. Also Luther's
much-abused dictum "peccare fortiter" is only the stormy outburst
of a man who has lived in constant fear of the law, who consumed
himself in unceasing efforts and tormenting, humiliating experiences
of "relapse," and who despaired at last of finding "justification" in
this way.[23] Criminals have often described the deep satisfaction, the
peace and liberation which they felt shortly after committing a deed
on which they had pondered for months, again and again repressing
their impulses while their minds became progressively more poisoned,
peaceless, and "evil."

In this respect as well, the Gospel's morality preserves its severely
individualistic character. The *salvation* and the *being* of the soul is its
primary concern. If indeed we follow the criterion of social utility, we
must judge and feel differently. Then the inner state of the individual
soul, especially of its unconscious layers, is unimportant: the main
thing is to keep the sinful impulse from harming the common interest.
Indeed an impulse is only "sinful" if it could lead to such harm. Jesus
judges differently: the sinner who sins is better than the sinner who
does not sin, but whose sinful impulse turns inward and poisons his
soul — even if the community is harmed by the former and not by
the latter. Thence his basic distrust, drawn from deep self-knowledge
— distrust not merely of the pharisee who only looks at his morally
well-trimmed social image, or of the Stoic who wants to be able to
"respect himself" and therefore does not look at his being, but at his

image as it appears in his self-judgment, but distrust even of him who decides only after "conscientious self-scrutiny" that he is "good" and "just." Even he may well bear the germs of sin within him, so that only the added sin of insufficient lucidity with respect to his own motives distinguishes him from the sinner who knows himself to be a sinner. In this context, St. Paul (I Cor. 4:3 and 4) sharply condemns not only all false "heteronomy," but also all Stoic and Kantian "autonomy" and all "self-judgment": "But with me it is a very small thing that I should be judged of you, or of man's judgment: yea, I judge not mine own self. [Indeed I could say] I know nothing by my self, yet I am not hereby justified: but he that judgeth me is the Lord." In this affection for the sinners we can find no *ressentiment*.[24]

Just as there are *two* ways of stooping lovingly to the weak, we can distinguish (among others) *two* sources of *ascetic* actions and value judgments. The ascetic ideal of life may be founded on an estrangement from one's body which can actually turn into hatred. I already indicated that this attitude is frequently the consequence of repressed impulses of hatred and revenge. This state of mind is often expressed in reflections such as "the body is the prison of the soul," and it can lead to diverse forms of bodily self-torture. Here again, the primary motive is not *love* of one's *spiritual* self and the wish to perfect and hallow it by disciplining the body. What is primary is *hatred of the body,* and the concern for "salvation of the soul" is a pretense which is often added only later. Another outgrowth of *ressentiment* are those forms of the ascetic ideal and its practice which are to justify one's impotence to acquire certain things — as when inability to do lucrative work leads to the imperative of poverty, erotic and sexual impotence to the precept of chastity, lack of self-discipline to obedience, etc. Nietzsche believes that the core of Christian asceticism can also be interpreted in this way.[25] In the ascetic ideal he sees the value reflex of a declining and exhausted life which secretly seeks death, even if its conscious will is different. Such life turns to ascetic values because they serve its hidden purpose. For Nietzsche, Christian asceticism as well falls under the rules and valuations which spring from *ressentiment.* Even virtues like the "toleration" of pain and misfortunes, and forgiveness and humility in the intercourse with others, are supposed to be due to *ressentiment*.[26]

But asceticism can have completely different origins and an entirely different meaning. It may simply serve the purpose of educating the citizens for certain fixed national goals, such as war or hunting. An example would be the strongly "ascetic" education in Sparta. This type of asceticism is entirely foreign to our context. There is a much higher and nobler form, which springs from vital plenitude, strength, and unity and derives meaning and value from life itself, from its glorification and greatest advancement, not from any transcendent goal. If this form of asceticism is to have any theoretical foundation, life must be viewed as an *autonomous* and *primary* agent, not reducible to mental phenomena (feelings, sensations), physical mechanisms, or a combination of both. Then inorganic matter and its mechanism is merely a medium for the representation and actualization of life, which is an organized structure of forms and functions. If we adopt this premise, then life also contains its own *values* which can never be reduced to utilitarian, hedonistic, or technical values.[27] Then the strongest life is not that which functions with a *maximum* of natural or artificially created mechanisms which are adapted to the surroundings, but a life which is still able to exist, grow, and even advance with a *minimum* of such mechanisms. In this case ascetic morality is the *expression* of *strong* life, and its rules are destined in turn to exercise and develop the purely vital functions with decreasing use of the necessary mechanisms.[28]

But when a hypothesis has the profundity of Nietzsche's speculation about the origin of Christian morality, it is not enough to reject it as false. We must also show how Nietzsche was led to his error and how it could gain for him such a high degree of probability.

There are two reasons. One is his *misjudgment* of the *essence of* Christian morality, notably of the Christian idea of love, in conjunction with the false standards by which he judges it (this last error is not historical and religious, but philosophical). The second reason lies in the factual *deformations* which Christian morality, starting with its early history, has undergone through reciprocal interchanges with values which have sprung from an entirely different historical background. These deformations often remained decisive for its future history.

There can be no doubt that the Christian ethos is inseparable from the Christian's *religious* conception of God and the world. It is meaningless without this foundation. There have been well-meaning attempts to invest it with a secular meaning which is separable from its religious significance, to discover in it the principles of a "humanistic" morality without religious premises. Such attempts, whether they are made by friends or foes of Christian religion, are fundamentally mistaken. At the very least, Christian morality must be tied to Christian religion by the assumption of a spiritual realm whose objects, contents, and values transcend not only the sensory sphere, but the whole sphere of *life*. This is precisely what Jesus calls the "kingdom of God." The precept of love is addressed to man as a *member* of the kingdom of God, where all are solidary. Even the feeling of unity and community, insofar as it does exist in the Christian world, refers to the kingdom of God or is at least founded in it.[29] However love, and the communion based on it, may work out in the secular forms of community, however much it may further our material welfare, free us from pain and create pleasure — all this is of value only if these communities, and the forces of love which cement them, have their living roots in the "kingdom of God" and refer back to it. This affirmation does not say to what degree the "kingdom of God" is represented either as "transcendent," "other-worldly," or as "immanent" and active in this world — to what degree it is represented as beginning after death or as always "present" and accessible to the pious. In any case it is conceived as a level of being — independent of the order, laws, and values of life — in which all the others are rooted and in which man finds the ultimate meaning and value of his existence.

If we fail to recognize this, then the Christian values — and all imperatives which spring from them — must be referred to a standard which, if valid, would indeed make them appear as values of decadence in the biological sense: the standard of what is most conducive to life. This is Nietzsche's interpretation. However, for the Christian, life — even in its highest form: human life — is never the "greatest good." Life, and therefore human society and history, is only important because it is the *stage* on which the "kingdom of God" must emerge. Whenever the preservation and advancement of life conflict with the realization of the values which exist in the kingdom of God, life becomes futile and is to be rejected, however valuable it may seem in itself. The body is not the "prison of the soul," as in Plato's dualism: it is the "temple of the holy Ghost" (I Cor. 6:19). Yet it is only a "temple" and does not constitute the ultimate value. Therefore it is said: "If thine eye offend thee, pluck it out ..." (Mark 9:47).

Love is not seen as a spiritual activity which *serves* life, nor as life's "strongest and deepest concentration" (Guyau). It is the activity and movement of love which embues life with its *highest meaning and value.* Therefore we can very well be asked to renounce life — and not only to sacrifice individual life for collective life, one's own life for somebody else's, or lower forms for higher forms of life: we can be asked to sacrifice life as such, in its very essence, if such an act would further the values of the kingdom of God, whose mystic bond and whose spiritual source of strength is love.[30] Nietzsche interprets Christianity from the outset as a mere "morality" with a religious "justification," not primarily as a "religion," and he applies to Christian values a standard which they themselves refuse consciously: the standard of the maximum quantity of life. Naturally he must conclude that the very postulation of a level of being and value which transcends life and is not relative to it must be the sign of a morality of decadence. This procedure, however, is completely arbitrary, philosophically wrong, and strictly refutable. The idea of goodness cannot be reduced to a biological value, just as little as the idea of truth. We must take this for granted here — the proof would lead too far.[31]

For the same reason, Nietzsche necessarily erred in another respect. If the Christian precepts and imperatives, especially those which refer to love, are detached from the kingdom of God and from man's spiritual personality by which he participates in this kingdom (not to be mistaken for his "soul," which is natural), there is another serious consequence: those postulates must enter in *constitutive* (not only accidental) conflict with all the laws which govern the development, growth, and expansion of life.

I insist that love for one's neighbor, in the Christian sense, is not originally meant to be a biological, political, or social principle.[32] It is directed — at least primarily — at *man's spiritual core,* his individual personality, through which alone he participates directly in the kingdom of God. Therefore Jesus is far removed from founding a new political order or a new economic distribution of property. He accepts the emperor's rule, the social distinction between master and slave,

and all those natural instincts which cause *hostility* between men in
public and private life. There is no idea of "general brotherhood," no
demand for a leveling of national distinctions through the creation
of a "universal community," corresponding to the Stoic ideal of a
"universal state" ("cosmopolites") and a universal law of reason and
nature. Nor is there any tendency to establish an independent Jewish
state or to realize any social and political utopia. The immanence of
the kingdom of God in man is not bound to any particular structure
of state and society.

The forces and laws which rule the evolution of life and the formation and development of political and social communities, even
wars[33] between nations, class struggle, and the passions they entail
— all those are taken for granted by Jesus as permanent factors of
existence. He does not want to replace them by love or anything else.
Such demands as universal peace or the termination of the social
power struggle are entirely foreign to his religious and moral sermon.
The "peace on earth" for which he asks is a profound state of blissful
quietude which is to permeate, as from above, the historical process
of struggle and conflict which governs the evolution of life and of human associations. It is a sacred region of peace, love, and forgiveness,
existing in the depth of man's soul in the midst of all struggle and
preventing him from believing that the goals of the conflict are ultimate
and definitive. Jesus does not mean that the struggle should cease and
that the instincts which cause it should wither away. Therefore the
paradoxical precept that one should love one's enemy is by no means
equivalent to the modern shunning of all conflict. Nor is it meant as
a praise of those whose instincts are too weak for enmity (Nietzsche
speaks of the "tamed modern gregarious animal")! On the contrary:
the precept of loving one's enemy presupposes the existence of hostility,
it accepts the fact that there are constitutive forces in human nature
which sometimes necessarily lead to hostile relations and cannot be
historically modified. It only demands that even the true and genuine
enemy — he whom I know to be my enemy and whom I am justified
in combating with all means at my disposal — should be my "brother
in the kingdom of God." In the midst of the struggle, *hatred* should
be absent, especially that *ultimate* hatred which is directed against
the salvation of his soul.[34] There is no value in the disappearance or

moderation of revenge, power, mastery, and subjugation which are acknowledged as belonging to a complete living being. The virtue lies in the free sacrifice of these impulses, and of the actions expressing them, in favor of the more valuable act of "forgiveness" and "toleration." Indeed one *cannot* "forgive" if one feels no revenge, nor can one "tolerate" if one is merely insensitive.[35]

Thus the greatest mistake would be to interpret the Christian movement on the basis of dim analogies with certain forms of the modern social and democratic movement. Jesus is *not* a kind of "popular hero" and "social politician," a man who knows what ails the poor and the oppressed, an "enemy of Mammon" in the sense that he opposes capitalism as a form of social existence. Yet Friedrich Nietzsche's own conception of Christianity is strongly influenced by this widespread Jesus picture, which was propagated by Christian and non-Christian socialists. Therefore he thinks that the motives and arguments which set him against modern Socialism and Communism also apply to Christian morality and its genius. But Nietzsche's attack touches Jesus and the core of Christianity as little as the praise of those "socialists," since both share the same mistaken premise. Christianity does not contain the germ of modern socialist and democratic tendencies and value judgments. Nor did it ever affirm the "equality of souls before God," to which Nietzsche always points as the root of democracy — except in the sense that God's judgment on men is preceded by an elimination of the value delusions which are due to human situations, to human narrow-mindedness, blindness, and self-interest. But the notion that all men are equivalent "in God's eyes," that all value distinctions and the whole value aristocracy of human existence are merely based on anthropomorphic prejudice, one-sidedness, and weakness, is reminiscent of Spinoza and entirely foreign to Christianity. It is in radical contradiction with ideas such as "heaven," "purgatory," "hell," and with the whole internally and externally *aristocratic* structure of Christian-ecclesiastic society — a structure which is continued and culminates in the invisible kingdom of God. The autochthonous Christian notion would rather be the opposite: that God sees an immeasurable abundance of differences and value distinctions where our eyes, fixed on outward appearances, see nothing but a seeming uniformity in the values of men, races, groups, and individuals. According to Pascal, even the human "spirit" is characterized by the ability to grasp the inner difference between men below their uniform appearance.

The communist organization of the original Christian communities does not prove any inner bond between Christian morality and the economic communism which is derived from democratic eudaemonism. This community of property was only the outward expression of the unity "of heart and soul" described in the Acts of the Apostles. Each individual was free to sell his houses and lands and to turn the proceeds over to the apostles, but there was no artificial and coercive expropriation, carried out by the state with the conscious purpose of guarantying general welfare. Nor was it believed that man's moral constitution could in any way be changed by the establishment of new property relations. Peter does not blame Ananias (cf. Acts 5:3 and 4) because he failed to turn over the full proceeds of his sale, but because he was "insincere" in pretending that the amount he brought to the apostle was the full amount. His property rights are explicitly acknowledged: "While it (i.e., the good) remained, was it not thine own? and after it was sold, was it not in thine own power?" This communism was founded on *voluntary* gifts, whose religious and moral value lay in the act of sacrificing and "giving." It was only an incidental phenomenon — due to the fact that all individuals happened to acknowledge the value of such behavior of their own free will. Moreover, the communism of these small early Christian circles applied to the fulfillment of needs, but not to the forms of production. Though they were surrounded by non-communist communities, they never indulged in any agitation which was to propagate their way of living or to extend it over the whole state. Therefore even this "social" twist given to the Christian idea of love, which was later called "caritas," everywhere presupposes the individualistic system of property.

We cannot fail to recognize this, except if we take the identity of the name for the identity of the thing. No Christian who was really inspired by the spirit of the Gospel has ever called for communism either for the sake of a "just" distribution of property, or as the natural and necessary result of a progressive interlocking of interests. Wherever Christian communism does appear, as in the forms of life of the monasteries, it is exclusively based on *free* acts of love and sacrifice.

The value of these acts lies in themselves alone and in the testimony they bear to the spiritual and religious freedom and elevation of the sacrificers as persons. Christian love and sacrifice *begins* where the demands of "justice" and the dictates of positive legislation end. Many modern philosophers[36] believe that the increase of legally justified demands makes voluntary love and sacrifice ever more superfluous. Such a view is diametrically opposed to Christian morality. Even when the law regulates a branch of social relief which used to be dependent on voluntary charity — as in the case of poor relief, which the state took over from the Churches and private individuals, or in modern German social legislation — this merely means that the Christian's love should turn to *wider, higher,* and *more spiritual* goals. It can never mean that love has become "superfluous" and is replaced by law and justice.

Christian love becomes visible in its purity where the mere interlocking of interests, which makes an action which is useful for A equally useful for B and C, *ceases* to function in favor of general welfare. Christian love is tied to the idea of a *definitive* "sacrifice," not a provisional one which ultimately enhances the quantity of pleasure in society.

Some philosophers, such as Herbert Spencer, believe that the "altruistic urge" (which they put in the place of love) will expand and "develop" through the increasing community of interests, and they posit an "ideal" goal[37] of development in which all kinds of "sacrifice" are eliminated. This urge, growing with the community of interests, has nothing at all to do with genuine "love."

# IV

# *Ressentiment* and Modern Humanitarian Love

Nietzsche ignored the fact that love in the Christian sense is always primarily directed at man's ideal spiritual self, at man as a member of the kingdom of God. Therefore he equated the Christian idea of love with a completely different idea which has quite another historical and psychological origin: *the idea and movement of modern universal love of man,* "humanitarianism," "love of mankind," or more plastically: "love toward every member of the human race." We agree with Nietzsche that *ressentiment* was the real root of this idea.

If we ignore the verbal similarity of the terms "Christian love" and "universal love of mankind" and concentrate on their respective significance and spiritual atmosphere, we feel that they represent entirely different *worlds.* First of all, modern humanitarianism is in every respect a polemical and protesting concept. It protests against divine love, and consequently against the Christian unity and harmony of divine love, self-love, and love of one's neighbor which is the "highest commandment" of the Gospel. Love is not to be directed at the "divine" essence in man, but only at man as such, outwardly recognizable as a member of his species, at him who "is a member of the human race."[1] This idea restricts love to the "human species," detaching it from all higher forces and values as well as from all other living beings and the rest of the world. "Man" is isolated not only from the "kingdom of God," but also from the non-human forms and forces of nature.[2] At the same time, the community of angels and souls is replaced by "mankind" as it exists at the moment — mankind as a visible, limited, earthly natural being. The Christian community of souls also includes the dead, i.e., *the whole of spiritually alive* humanity, organized according to the aristocracy of its moral merits and personal values. Thus the real object of love extends into visible contemporary mankind insofar as divine spiritual life has germinated in it, but is much wider and greater and is always accessible in a living interchange of prayer, intercession, and veneration. "Love of mankind" is also polemical against (and devoid of piety toward) the love and veneration of the *dead,* the men of the past, and the *tradition* of their spiritual values and volitions in every form. Its object undergoes yet another change: the "neighbor" and the "individual," who alone represents humanity in its depth of personality, is replaced by "mankind" as a *collective entity.* All love for a part of mankind — nation, family, individual — now appears as an unjust *deprivation* of what we owe only to the totality. It is characteristic that Christian terminology knows no "love of mankind." Its prime concept is "love of one's neighbor." It is primarily directed at the person and at certain spiritually valuable acts — and at "man" only to the degree that he is a "person" and accomplishes these acts, i.e., to the degree to which he realizes the order of the "kingdom of God." It is directed at the "neighbors," the "nearest" visible beings who are alone capable of that deeper penetration into the layer of spiritual personality which is the highest form of love. Modern humanitarian love, on the other hand, is only interested in the *sum total* of human individuals. Bentham's principle that each individual should count for one, and none for more than one, is only a conscious formulation of the implicit tendency of modern "humanitarianism." Therefore all love for a *more restricted* circle here appears *a priori* as a *deprivation* of the rights due to the wider circle — without any reference to such questions as value and "nearness to God." Thus patriotism is supposed to deprive "mankind," etc.[3]

The difference between Christian love and modern humanitarianism lies not only in their objects, but also in the *subjective* side of the process of loving. Christian love is essentially a spiritual *action* and *movement,* as independent of our body and senses as the acts and laws of thinking. Humanitarian love is a *feeling,* and a passive one, which arises primarily by means of psychical contagion when we perceive the outward expression of pain and joy. We suffer when we see pain and rejoice when we see pleasant sensations. In other words, we do not even suffer in sympathy with the other person's suffering as such, but only with our sense perception of his pain. It is no coincidence that the philosophical and psychological theoreticians of the 17th and 18th centuries, who gradually elaborated the theoretical formulation of the new ethos, define the essence of love with reference to the phenomena of sympathy, compassion, and shared joy, which in turn they reduce to psychical contagion.[4] This goes particularly for the great English thinkers from Hutcheson, Adam Smith, David Hume to Bain, and also for Rousseau.[5] The pathos of modern humanitarianism, its clamor for greater sensuous happiness, its subterraneous-ly smoldering passion, its revolutionary protest against all institutions, traditions, and customs which it considers as obstacles to the increase of sensuous happiness, its whole revolutionary spirit — all this is in characteristic contrast to the luminous, almost cool *spiritual enthusiasm* of Christian love. It should not surprise us that psychological theory, following this historical change in experiencing love, increasingly dissolves the very phenomenon of love into a mechanism of necessary delusions. Sometimes sympathy is reduced to the act of artificially putting oneself in another's place — according to the question: "What would you feel if this happened to you?" — and of reproducing the feelings we ourselves experienced at analogous occasions. Sometimes (as by Bain) it is reduced to a kind of hallucination of feeling, in which we are violently drawn into the other person's state of mind, as if we momentarily underwent the sufferings we see. Then again, it is explained as an "empathy" through the reproduction of one's own previous experiences; this reproduction is supposed to be directly prompted by the imitation of the other person's expressions of emotion, so that we need not "put ourselves in his place."[6] Finally, sympathy may be interpreted as the mere mental correlative of certain fixed and primary impulses to act which are useful for the species — i.e., as a consequence of the gregarious instinct, which can be observed even in the animal kingdom.[7] Thus in theory as well, love descends step by step from its exalted place as token and symbol of an order which transcends the natural, indeed as the *moving force* within the kingdom of God. It becomes an animal drive which continually grows in refinement and complexity through man's social evolution and intellectual development. Starting from the sexual sphere, it becomes ever more richly *specialized* and tends to spread over wider and wider areas. Spencer and Darwin were the thinkers who finally formulated this reduction of love's loftiest expressions to the instinct of furthering the species, existing already in animal societies. The reduction presupposes a complete misunderstanding of the *nature* of these phenomena, and it was possible only after the *historical movement itself* had evolved certain feelings — and a concomitant idea — whose psychological core may indeed not be essentially different from the mentality of gregarious animals.[8]

Finally, the *valuation* of "universal love of mankind" has a foundation which widely differs from that of love in Christian morality. The value of love is not supposed to lie in the *salvation* of the lover's soul as a member of the kingdom of God, and in the ensuing contribution to the salvation of others, but in the advancement of "general *welfare.*" Love is merely the X in emotional life which leads to generally useful acts, or the *"disposition"* for such emotions. It has positive value only insofar as it has this possible *value of effectiveness.* The best world, in the Christian perspective, would be the world with a *maximum* of love, even if that love were unaccompanied by insight in the state of mind of others (i.e., the ability to "understand" others) and in the natural and social *causal relations* which are indispensable if love is to effect useful rather than detrimental actions. In the modern perspective, humanitarian love itself is only one of the causal factors which can augment the general welfare. But what if we object that other feelings and instincts — such as the instinct of self — preservation, the sexual urge, jealousy, lust for power, vanity — advance "welfare" and its development much *more* than love?[9] The defender of modern humanitarianism can only answer that the value of love is not exclusively determined by the insignificant amount of usefulness it creates — after all, narcotics, the antiseptic dressing of wounds, and similar inventions have allayed much more pain and dried many more tears than love! Love is also valuable because it is so much *rarer* than these other instincts. It needs augmenting — an aim which is furthered in turn by its social prestige. If the "altruistic" urges (which supposedly coincide with "love") should ever happen to prevail quantitatively over the egoistic inclinations, then the latter would be more highly esteemed.

It hardly needs stating that this "theory" is in complete contradiction with the *evident* meaning of our valuation of love.

The profound inner difference between the facts and concepts of Christian and those of humanitarian love seems to have escaped Nietzsche completely. He failed to realize that everywhere many *demands* made in the name of humanitarian love were different from the spirit of Christian love and often diametrically opposed to it. The highly Christian period of the Middle Ages, during which Christian love reached its purest flowering as an idea and form of life, saw no contradiction between this principle and the feudal aristocratic hierarchy of secular and ecclesiastical society, including bondage. It was able to accept such phenomena as the contemplative life of the monks, which was hardly "generally useful"[10]; the numerous formations of territorial states and rules, the countless local customs; the rigorous discipline in education; war, knighthood, and the system of values based on them; the qualified death penalty, torture, and the whole cruel penal code; even the Inquisition and the autodafés. In fact, the judgments of the Inquisition were decreed "in the name of love" — not merely love for the community of true believers who might be poisoned by the heretic and deprived of their salvation, but love for the heretic himself. Through the burning of his body, his soul was to be specially commended to God's grace. This intentionality of love was entirely sincere, though from our point of view it is based on *superstition.* Thus all these facts were quite compatible with the principle of Christian love,[11] and some of them were actually justified in its name, as means to educate men to Christian love (though in part, of course, with superstitious premises). Yet in the name of the universal love of mankind they are rejected, fought, and overthrown. Humanitarian love is from the outset an egalitarian force which demands the dissolution of the feudal and aristocratic hierarchy, of all forms of bondage and personal subjection, and the abolition of the "idle" and useless monastic orders. For Bossuet it was still evident that patriotism is preferable to love of mankind, since the values invested in one's native country are of an essentially higher order than those which all men hold in common. Now it appears evident that the value of love grows with its range. Here too, the quantitative criterion replaces the qualitative one. "Universal love of mankind" becomes progressively more powerful until the French Revolution, when one head after another was struck off "in the name of mankind." It demands the removal of national and territorial "blinkers," the political and finally even the socio-economic equality of all men, the standardization of life in customs and usages, and a more "humane" and uniform system of education. It increasingly calls for universal peace and bitterly fights all those forms of life and value judgments which spring from knighthood and indeed from the whole caste of warriors. The alleviation of the penal code, the abolition of torture and of the qualified death penalty are demanded in its name. To its representatives, the Inquisition is nothing but insult and mockery, directed against the very essence of the commandment of love — not an institution based on superstition. The attitude toward the poor, the sick, and the morally evil undergoes a fundamental change as well. Modern humanitarianism does not command and value the *personal* act of love from man to man, but primarily the impersonal *"institution"* of welfare. This is not the exuberance of a life that *bestows* blissfully and lovingly, overflowing out of its abundance and inner security. It is an involvement, through psychical contagion, in the feeling of depression that is manifested in outward expressions of pain and poverty. The purpose of the helping deed is to remove this specifically modern phenomenon of "sham pity," of "feeling sorry."[12] Christian "mercy" (note the force and spirit of this old-fashioned word) is replaced by the feeling expressed in the statement "it arouses my pity"![13] As early as 1787, Goethe could question the kind of "humanism" *(Humanität)* Herder preached under Rousseau's influence: "Moreover .... I think it is true that humanism will triumph at last; only I fear that the world will at the same time be a vast hospital, where each will be his fellow man's humane sick-nurse."[14] The movement of modern humanitarianism found its first powerful literary expression in Rousseau — often, indeed, concealed in this great mind's rich and multifarious preoccupations, but quite evidently propelled by the fire of a gigantic *ressentiment*. His ideas are presented so suggestively. that scarcely one great German of that time, except for Goethe, escaped the contagious power of Rousseau's pathos (for example, Fichte, Herder, Schiller, Kant all have their Rousseauistic phase). Humanitarianism found its philosophical expression and clear formulation chiefly in the positivistic circles, starting with Auguste

Comte, who puts "mankind" as "Grand-Etre" in the place of God.[15] Its most repugnant manifestations — which in reality only develop the original germs of the idea — are the modern realist "social" novel, the dramatical and lyrical poetry of sickness and morbidity, and the modern "social" administration of justice.

Friedrich Nietzsche lived in a period when precisely these extreme formulations and products of "modern humanitarianism" were gaining consideration and applause. This explains his struggle against the whole movement.

For in our opinion he is *right* in interpreting this idea, and especially the way in which it developed in the modern social movement — but *not* the Christian idea of love! — as a historical accumulation of *ressentiment,* growing through tradition. He rightly sees in it a symptom and expression of descending life. The humanitarian movement is in its essence a *ressentiment* phenomenon, as appears from the very fact that this socio-historical emotion is by no means based on a spontaneous and original *affirmation of a positive value,* but on a *protest, a counter-impulse* (hatred, envy, revenge, etc.) against ruling minorities that are known to be in the possession of positive values. "Mankind" is not the immediate object of love (it cannot be, for love can be aroused only by concrete objects) — it is merely a *trump card* against a hated thing. Above all, this love of mankind is the expression of a repressed rejection, of a counter-impulse against God.[16] It is the disguised form of a repressed hatred of God. Again and again it proclaims that there is "not enough love in the world" for wasting it on non-human beings — a typical *ressentiment* statement. Bitterness against the idea of the highest lord, inability to bear the "all-seeing eye," impulses of revolt against "God" as the symbolic unity and concentration of all positive values and their rightful domination — all these are *primary* components of humanitarian love. "Lovingly" stooping to man as a *natural being* — that is the *second* step! Man is loved because his pain, his ills and sufferings in themselves form a gladly accepted objection against God's "wise and benevolent rule." Wherever I find historical evidence of this feeling, I also detect a secret satisfaction that the divine rule can be impugned.[17] Since the positive values are anchored in the idea of God through the power of tradition — a tradition even non-believers cannot escape — it inevitably follows that this *"humanitarian* love," based as it is on protest and rejection, becomes primarily directed at the *lowest,* the *animal* aspects of human nature. These, after all, are the qualities which "all" men clearly have in common. This tendency is still unmistakable in the terms we use to point out a person's "humanity." We rarely do this when he has done something good and reasonable, or something which *distinguishes* him — usually we want to defend him against a reproach or an accusation: "He is only human," "We are all human," "To err is human," etc. This emotional tendency is typical for modern humanitarianism. A man who is nothing and has nothing is still a "human being." The very fact that love is directed at the *species* implies that it is essentially concerned with the inferior qualities which must be "understood" and "excused." Who can fail to detect the secretly glimmering *hatred* against the positive higher values, which are *not* essentially tied to the "species" — a hatred hidden deep down below this "mild," "understanding," "humane" attitude?

"Universal love of mankind" has sprung from *ressentiment* in yet another *dual* sense. First, as a manifestation of inner protest and aversion against the immediate *circle* of the community and its inherent values — against the "community" which has physically and mentally formed a man. Experience shows very frequently that children who vainly sought their parents' tenderness, who felt "out of place" at home for some reason, or whose love was rejected, expressed their inner *protest* through intense enthusiasm for "mankind." Here again, this vague and confused enthusiasm is due to repressed *hatred* of the family and the immediate surroundings.[18] On a historical scale, this is the source of the love of "mankind," the "cosmopolitan" affect, which is so noticeable in the writings of the later Stoics[19]: it spread in the aging Roman Empire when the individual, severed from the nourishing and sustaining force of the city state, felt lonely and deprived of all support. Exactly the same motive underlies "modern humanitarian love." It came about mainly as a *protest against patriotism* and finally turned into a protest against every organized community. Thus it is the secondary result of a repressed hatred of one's native country.[20]

Finally, the *ressentiment* character of modern humanitarianism is also proved by the fact that its leading spokesmen (for example, Auguste Comte) describe it as "altruism." For the Christian conception of love, devotion to one's fellow man merely because he is the "other" is as false and misplaced as the liberal-individualistic idea that we best serve the whole and the community by perfecting ourselves — according to the saying: "When the rose adorns itself, it adorns the garden."[21] In the Christian view, love is an act of a particular quality, directed at the *ideal spiritual person* as such, and it makes no difference whether it is the person of the lover or that of the "other." That is why the Christian considers it sinful to renounce one's "salvation" for somebody else's sake! And therefore his own "salvation" is as important to him as love of his neighbor. "Love God and thy neighbor as thyself," is the Christian precept. It is characteristic that a leading spokesman of modern humanitarianism, Auguste Comte — the inventor of the term "altruism," which is a barbarism — takes offense at this postulate. He accuses Christianity of aiding and abetting "egoistic impulses" because it commands us to care for our own salvation as well, and he wants to replace this precept by the new positivistic commandment: "Love thy neighbor *more* than thyself." He fails to see that Christian "love" is a particular kind of spiritual act, which is by its very essence primarily oriented toward the spiritual person (of God and men), and toward the body merely as its vessel and "temple." Thus the relation to the other is not an essential characteristic of Christian love, and Christianity necessarily knows a "self-love" which is basically different from all "egoism." Comte fails to note that it is incomprehensible why our fellow man should have a right to benefaction — since love, for Comte, has value only as a "cause" for good deeds — for the silliest of reasons: simply because he is the "other." If I myself am not worthy of love, why should the *"other"* be? As if he were not also an "I" — for himself, and I "another" — for him! Comte ignores that his tenet is either a hyperbolical pathetic phrase or a nihilistic demand which destroys all vitality and indeed decomposes any structure of being! But the real question is how such a demand is psychologically explicable.

There is a delusion which consists in mistaking for love what is really a peculiar sham form of love, founded on *self-hatred* and *self-flight*. In his *Pensées*, Blaise Pascal has drawn the classic picture of a type of man who is entangled in many worldly activities (games, sports, hunting, also "business" or unceasing work for the "community"), and all this merely because he cannot look at himself and continually tries to escape from the vacuum, from his feeling of nothingness. In some psychoses, for example, in hysteria, we find a kind of "altruism" in which the patient has become incapable of feeling and experiencing anything "by himself." All his experiences are sympathetic, built on those of *another* person and *his* possible attitude and expectation, *his* possible reaction to any event. The patient's own existence has lost its center and focus, he neglects all his affairs, is completely drawn into the "other's" life — and suffers from it. He eats nothing or injures himself in order to vex the "other." In a milder form, the same phenomenon occurs in the movement of "universal humanitarian love." This attitude sometimes takes the form of a collective delusion, as within the Russian intelligentsia, especially the academic youth of both sexes, which likes to inject its morbid urge for self-sacrifice and self-flight into social and socio-political "goals" and then interprets its morbidity as "moral heroism."[22] The "social politician" who troubles his head about everything except himself and his own business (a type now increasingly frequent) is usually nothing but a poor and empty human being fleeing from himself.[23] Nietzsche is perfectly right in pointing out that this way of living and feeling is morbid, a sign of *declining* life and hidden nihilism, and that its "superior" morality is pretense. His criticism, however, does not touch the Christian love of one's neighbor: it does touch an essential component of modern "love of mankind," which is in effect fundamentally a socio-psychological phenomenon of degeneration.

The Christian idea of love is a superior spiritual principle organizing human life. Though the strengthening of life is not its affirmed goal, it is in fact an expression of "ascending" life. But the effeminate sensuous feeling indiscriminate sympathy for the "other" — and mainly for his "suffering" — merely because he is not oneself is a highly leveling and decomposing principle for human life, despite its express purpose of "strengthening life." At the same time, it is an *expression* of declining life. "Modern humanitarian love" degrades itself to the level of a mere technical value, an instrument for the attainment of general welfare. This is indeed an unheard-of "falsification of the tablets of value" since the immense value of love, and the bliss connected with its act, is thus subordinated to any sensuous pleasure — independent of the *value* of the person who enjoys it. The great lovers, the most sacred phenomena of history, in whom — according to the Christian view — the kingdom of God becomes visible, are no longer the surpassing examples and the lasting *models* for "mankind," those whose very existence somewhat justifies and also elevates the human "species." They now appear as mere ministrants to the multitude, serving to enhance its pleasure! This is truly and literally a "slave revolt" in morality! Not a revolt of the "slaves," but of the slavish *values*.

However much the *ideas* of Christian and humanitarian love may differ in substance and origin, in concrete historical practice they have entered many complex *alliances* which explain Niet-zsche's mistake, though they do not justify it. The same is true of the numerous forms of asceticism.

Even before the emergence of the specifically modern idea of humanism, at the time of the constitution of the universal Church, the ideology of the later Stoics merged with the Christian conception of love. As the Church opened its gates more widely and became more universal, the ideas of cosmopolitanism, natural law, and natural morality were introduced into its doctrine and philosophy — not so much for their positive substance as for their usefulness in the struggle *against* the power of the states, of national and territorial customs and legislation.[24] The leveling, decomposing principle of the new "love of mankind" partly penetrated into Christian ideology.[25] At the same time, the love of God obtained a eudaemonistic slant.[26]

But the more Christian morality in life and philosophy appears in its purity, the less I find the notion that the human *species* has a *uniform* spiritual structure, and the assumption that the disposition for salvation is everywhere *identical*. *The* idea of an "equality of rational potentialities" is as foreign to the genuine Christian doctrine as it is to true antiquity.[27] In the view of the ancients, as it is sharply formulated by Aristotle, the difference between slaves and free men is "natural," and the legal distinctions between the classes are to reflect this original inequality as adequately as possible. Thus it is false to interpret legal inequality as the imperfect expression of an underlying ideal of *equal* natural rights, which is perverted by factual power relations. Quite the contrary, every factual legal equality conceals a basic inequality of rightful claims which is founded on the unchangeable natural difference between "slaves" and "free men." It is only due to the subjective and technical difficulty of recognizing these essential qualities, and of establishing a unity of defining characteristics which reflects them, that they cannot always find expression in *positive* law. For the ancients it is axiomatic that equal rights are in any case unjust. Only opportunism can bring them about, and they always conceal a "just" inequality of rightful claims by the different groups. It is true that Christianity destroys this point of view, but only by making an even greater qualitative distinction between men, which penetrates much more deeply into the ontological depths of the person. For the ancients, man is separated from the animal by the faculty of reason. The new Christian criterion goes far beyond this distinction and makes it appear relatively unimportant. The Christian distinction is that between the "state of nature" and the "state of grace," between "carnal" and "reborn" man. The line of separation runs between him who is in a state of "eternal life," who is "a child of the kingdom of God," and him who has not attained this state. Augustine gave the most extreme formulation, which was later rejected by the Church precisely because of the growing Stoical and rational component of its ideology: he spoke of the "reprobate" and the "elect." In the early Christian view, the difference between the "carnal and natural man" and the animal is only one of *degree,* not one of kind. A *new* order, a new absolute layer of being, appears only in the "reborn man." He represents a new *kind* of life and being, which puts him above man and beast, whereas reason is merely a higher development of natural potentialities which also exist in the animal kingdom. The idea that each human being has a "spiritual, rational, immortal soul" with equal potentialities, equal claims for salvation, or even equal "abilities" or "innate ideas," and that by virtue of this fact alone (without "grace," "revelation," "rebirth") man is essentially superior to the animal and to the rest of nature — this whole notion was added to Christian ideology at an early date, but has not grown from its living roots.[28] It is originally introduced not as a "truth," but as a mere *pragmatic-pedagogic* assumption, indispensable for rendering missionary work possible and meaningful. For exactly the same reason, ancient logic and dialectics — first rejected as "diabolical" — became the chief subjects of instruction in ecclesiastical philosophy.[29] In order to reconcile his doctrine of grace with his priestly practice, Augustine writes that nobody can know whether a person is an "elect" or a "reprobate," neither he himself nor any priest, so that the practical priest must treat *every* man "as if" he were not a reprobate. But though originally a pedagogic and pragmatic assumption, the doctrine of the equality of human nature lays more and more claim to being considered as a metaphysical *truth*.

It is remarkable that the original Christian view corresponds to the modern theory of evolution precisely on this essential point. It agrees that "man as such is only a more highly developed animal," with the qualification that this applies only to the man who has not become a member of the "kingdom of God." Nietzsche's attempt at establishing an essential qualitative distinction between men — the distinction between "degenerate animal" and "superman" — does not in itself separate him from genuine Christianity. The only difference lies in his positive answer, which sees the superman as a new "type" to be created by an act of will, instead of being constituted by participation in the kingdom of God. But he shares his "anti-humanism" with true Christian morality. Here again, the Church has ended up by making metaphysical *truths* of mere pragmatic *maxims* which were first adopted for their usefulness in mission work and the guidance of souls, in governing the Church and establishing its unity. The *ressentiment* rationalism and humanism of the modern bourgeoisie then remained an element of Church ideology, even at the time of its greatest flowering, however much it kept them within bounds. By his destruction of "natural theology," his hatred of reason, his opposition and struggle against the scholastic attempts to rationalize Christian ideas, Luther shows how dearly he distinguished the genuine elements from the peripheral additions — in contrast to Melanchthon, the "praeceptor Germaniae." But Luther denied that love, like faith, is an original force transcending the natural domain, and he included even the inner act of love in the sphere of the "works"[30] which are no true road to salvation. Thus he disavowed the Christian idea of love even *more deeply* than the institution he attacked, and even more strongly than the Church he prepared the modern "humanistic" idea which sees in love a purely human, carnal, sensuous force.[31] Luther completely destroys the moral-religious basis of the *principle of solidarity*.[32] Love of others is now subordinated to self-love, but without awareness. Luther believes that the genuine and "mere" faith in Jesus' expiatory death will make us aspire for the "awareness of a merciful God," for the "awareness of justification and atonement," for the most profound inner peace. But how could these aspirations arise without an act of love toward oneself and the consequent care for one's own salvation? Luther excludes the love of others as a necessary road to justification — he founds it on justification already won through faith "alone," in each soul's *private* communication with its God. However, since the craving for justification is factually based on self-love, the love of others is completely subordinated to self-love and is ultimately reduced to mere *sensuous instinctive sympathy* among men. The process of salvation takes place exclusively between each soul and "its" God. It is denied on principle that the living *community* in faith and love is equally necessary, as the scene for the process of salvation. This destroys the very basis of the idea that the *Church* is the institution of salvation.[33] The legal and moral organization of the community must now be entirely left to the state alone ("the authorities") or to natural instincts — without any possible reference to a spiritual moral authority which renounces all worldly power on principle. It is true that all the blunders and mistakes (from indulgence to autodafé) by which the pre-reformatory Church often "provided" for salvation have thus become impossible. Yet this has only been attained by renouncing the very principle of an inner community which reaches into the sphere of the kingdom of God itself, for this principle requires as much love and care for the fellow man's salvation for one's own.[34] The act of Christian love of oneself and of others is the deepest root of Christian morality. By excluding it from the essential factors of the "road to salvation," Luther separates religion from morality. Love becomes a mere human force, founded on natural sympathy, and the modern positivist idea of humanism and love of mankind is indirectly prepared for in a powerful way.

The Christian conception of love was even more completely distorted by the positive alliances with the *modern* idea of humanitarian love into which all the Christian denominations entered to an increasing degree. These alliances were so close that not only people of average education, but even many contemporary theologians failed to see the radical difference between these ideas and mingled them into that unsavory brew of unprincipled "love" for everybody which rightly aroused Nietzsche's disgust and criticism. Even much earlier, great men of good taste such as Kant were thus led to the comprehensible error of denying that love is a moral agent.[35]

This turbid mixture occurred, in characteristic form, in all the types and variations of so-called "Christian socialism" and "Christian democracy." In the Catholic countries, these tendencies appeared after the French Revolution and after the Church had made its peace with democracy, and they gained momentum when the Church began to use the socialist organizations and the democratic mass movements for its own purposes. Both the modern, specifically democratic variation of ultramontanism and the Protestant social movement are products and expressions of this amalgamation of ideas. All attempts to derive "socio-political programs" from Christian morality, new principles for the division of property and power, have flowed from this turbid amalgamation of utilitarianism and Christian morality. After the preceding remarks, it will hardly be necessary to point out that this intermingling of Christian love with social and economic interests is highly reprehensible from the standpoint of true Christian love. Indeed, those forms of socialism which do not seek their victory in "humanism" or "love," but in the one-sided organization of purely *economic interests* and in an honest *struggle* between the classes, are highly superior in the moral sense. These groups may more or less have lost their Christianity, but in their own way they respect it more deeply than those who want to avoid the class struggle and to make "love" a socio-political principle. For the latter deform its core, and wherever they prevail, they prevent those who have lost Christianity from ever retrieving it. Christian morality forbids class *hatred,* but not an honest class *struggle* which is conscious of its goals. Therefore the dictum of Emperor William II about the "social ministers" is extremely pertinent and striking in its brevity: "Protestant-social is nonsense; whoever is Protestant is also social."[36]

It seems to me beyond doubt that Nietzsche was thinking of these mixtures of ideas when he equated such dissimilar moral views as that of Comte's positivism and that of Christian love, declaring both *without distinction* to be forms of a morality of "descending life," a "slave morality." But he failed to see that those moral currents in the contemporary Christian Churches that are really signs of descending life, based on *ressentiment,* have this character only because of their turbid *amalgamation* with specifically modern ideas, especially with the modern democratic idea of humanism. Therefore Nietzsche made the fundamental mistake of considering these modern ideas and movements as *consequences* of Christian morality! Strangely enough, he thought that the growing vulgarization and deformation of true Christianity, its defeat by modern civilization, was equivalent with *genuine* Christian morality — indeed that Christianity was the "source" of that civilization!

The "ascetic ideals" which have entered Christianity must be seen in an analogous way. There is only one form of asceticism which has sprung from the roots of Christian morality. It is that asceticism which serves primarily to *liberate* the spiritual personality, secondarily to exercise the vital functions independently of the mechanisms that serve them, so that the living being becomes largely *independent* of momentary external stimuli. All other types of asceticism are not of Christian origin. This goes for all asceticism founded on *hatred* and *contempt* for the body, and also for asceticism as a means for attaining a "type of cognition" which overcomes the "personal" form of life, allowing us to merge mystically with "non-personal being." The same can be said of those forms of asceticism which extend the demand of abstention to the *spiritual* goods of civilization and their enjoyment, or which want to subject even the "soul" to an arbitrary "discipline" where thoughts, feelings, and sensations are treated as soldiers who can be arrayed at will for certain "purposes." All these types of asceticism, when found in the Christian sphere, are associations of Christian morality with the *ressentiment* of dying antiquity, especially of Neo-Platonism and Essenianism, or else (as the "asceticism" inaugurated by Ignatius of Loyola) an entirely modern technique of "submission to authority" that has no specific goal, but merely extends the military idea of "discipline" and "blind obedience" to the ego's relations with its thoughts, aspirations, and feelings.[37]

It is certainly true that the history of Christianity shows terrible instances of contempt of the body, especially of the sexual impulse. But the core of Christian theory and practice remained *free* from those phenomena. The notion of the "resurrection of the flesh" sanctifies the flesh and the idea of the "body," introducing it into the kingdom of God itself. Christian philosophy as well remained basically free from the "dualism" of soul and body. Thus for Thomas Aquinas, the "soul" as animating principle of the body and as a spiritual force forms *one* indivisible *unity*. Only in modern philosophy (Descartes etc.) there appears that new attitude, prepared by certain Franciscan theories, according to which the "thinking ego," severed from all its vital foundations, looks down upon the active "body" as if it were just an external *object* among others.[38]

The purpose of Christian asceticism, when it was not influenced by the Hellenistic philosophy of decadence, was by no means the suppression or even extirpation of the natural instincts, but merely their *control* and their complete *spiritualization*. It is positive, not negative asceticism, essentially concerned with liberating the highest forces of the personality from blockage by the automatism of the lower instincts.[39]

It is quite ridiculous to hold up "serene Greek monism of life" against "gloomy and dismal Christian asceticism." For the asceticism which deserves this name is precisely "Greek" and "Hellenistic." The feeling that the body as such is "sordid," a "fountain of sin," a confinement to be overcome, a "dungeon," etc., has its source in the decline of antiquity. From there, it sometimes penetrated into the Christian Church. Christian asceticism is serene and gay; it is a gallant awareness of one's power to control the body! Only the "sacrifice" made for the sake of a *higher positive* joy is agreeable to God!

V

# *Ressentiment* and Other Value Shifts
# in Modern Morality

Hitherto we have traced only one fundamental value of modern "morality" to the forces of *ressentiment:* "universal love of mankind." The falsifying activity of *ressentiment* will now be shown in the case of three *other* basic elements of that "morality." We select three elements which we consider to be particularly important, knowing well that this choice does not suffice to characterize adequately (and still less to exhaust) modern morality. Moreover, our discussion must remain confined to the perversion of principles — we cannot demonstrate how this perversion governs the concrete process of valuation in the various domains of value. The author has gathered rich material for such an enterprise, but it will have to be reserved for future publication.[1]

## 1. THE VALUE OF THINGS
## SELF-EARNED OR SELF-ACQUIRED

We begin by citing a rule of preference which has come to determine the morality of the modern world: *Moral value pertains only to those qualities, actions, etc., which the individual has acquired by his own strength and labor.* According to this view, there are no specific original "dispositions" of moral value — on the contrary, these are opposed to the morally valuable qualities as mere "natural gifts," for example by Kant. Nor are there particular "gifts of grace," *virtutes infusae,* and "calls" which could elevate one person above another. There is no hereditary good or hereditary guilt[2] — neither in a Christian

— ecclesiastic nor in any other sense! "Hereditary good" and "hereditary guilt" are contradictions in terms if the above determination is accepted. Neither antiquity nor Christianity knew this valuation, which severs moral value and the meaning of life from all inner connections with the universe, with biological origin, history, and even God, and wants to build it on nothing but the individual's solitary and limited strength.

The ultimate reason for this new valuation is a *different attitude in apprehending values.* When I see a man who naturally has superior ability and excellence, I will prefer him to the man who must work hard to acquire these qualities, provided that my attention and feeling are oriented toward the *values themselves.* I will happily and gratefully acknowledge the fact that the former already has what the latter must acquire and is therefore closer to the ideal of perfection. *How* he obtained it is a different question! He, after all, who sets out on life's journey with greater moral talents can through effort attain a higher level than the less gifted. But when the poorer and lower nature *cannot bear* this original distance from the superior one and *suffers* from the comparison, then this ungrudging ability to see and accept the better "nature" (or "grace," when the premises are religious) is supplanted by an entirely different attitude! Then the previously described mechanism of *ressentiment* sets in, with the tendency to deny the moral value of this advantage. All value is now attached to "work," which is supposed to raise the moral level. The value of the initial and final level plays no role. The emphasis no longer lies on the evident objective *qualities* of value, but on the subjective process of "work." The result is the following axiom: "There is moral value only in that which *everyone* — even the least gifted — can do." All human beings now appear "equal" in moral value and talents — "equal" in the sense that the moral level of the *least* gifted sets the criterion. The higher and richer "nature" is dispossessed by this new principle of judging, it is deprived of its rights by the statement that its gifts are not due to its own merit and are therefore without the slightest moral value. Conversely, the new principle enhances the self-confidence of the "have-not" in the moral sphere, the moral "proletarian" as it were. What he could not bear, the surpassing importance of the "superior nature," has now been fundamentally devaluated. The sweat and tears of his moral "toil" are now shining in the light of highest value! Through this transvaluation, his secret thirst for revenge against the better man has now been quenched.[3]

The motive behind this transvaluation has nothing whatever to do with the presumed realization that moral values — in contrast with others, such as aesthetic values — must be based on free acts.[4] This is shown by the fact that the same shift takes place in extramoral domains of value, in legal and economic life. The theories of property and value of the English political and economic theoreticians, first John Locke and then Adam Smith and David Ricardo, merely formulate and conceptualize an existent tendency of modern valuation. They hold that the right of ownership as well is derived from *labor* on the objects, not from occupation or other origins. It is clear that this new standard must lead to a most radical critique of the existing systems of ownership insofar as they can be historically traced back to occupation, war,[5] donations, primogeniture, etc. Indeed with this premise, the entire law of succession is disputable *in principle,* wherever it cannot be justified as a merely technical means for the distribution of things which ensures maximum usefulness. But just as all moral activity takes place within the framework of moral *existence,* all labor on objects *presupposes* their ownership — the aims, organization, techniques, and forms of labor are historically dependent On the systems of ownership and change with them.[6]

Who cannot see that this "theory" has sprung from the laboring classes' *envy of* groups that did not acquire their property through work? The right of ownership of the latter is declared to be illusory, or merely the consequence of an illegal situation which one has a "right" to shake off.

The theory of labor *value* is analogous. There are original value distinctions between the materials in the goods, which vary with the nature of the country. The *formal* values of the goods are independent of "labor," they are due to the inventiveness of resourceful persons who set *models* for labor. Another value lies in the combination of the results of labor which is brought about by the activity of the coordinator and supervisor. Yet all these values are now disregarded from the outset, or they are to be converted into the currency of "labor" — in order to found the senseless tenet that each has a right to a quantity of values *equal* to that which he has produced by his "labor" (the so-called "right to the whole product of labor").

Two other basic rules are closely connected with the above: first, the *denial of human solidarity* in moral guilt and merit, which is the premise of Christian valuation; second, the *assumption of the equality of men* with regard to their spiritual and moral potentialities (Descartes, Locke).[7]

The reduction of moral value to that which is "self-acquired" entails the notion that a person's moral value is limited to the things he does "by himself." Concepts like "hereditary guilt," "hereditary good," "participation in the moral merits of the saints," and "common guilt" become meaningless combinations of words.

The notion of a *moral solidarity*[8] of mankind appears not only in ideas such as "we all sinned in Adam" and "we were all resurrected in Jesus," but also in the notion that we should feel we participate in all guilt (which is more than merely "remembering" our own guilt). Moreover, everyone shares in the merits of the saints, and the "poor souls" can be redeemed by the moral works of posterity. There are many notions of this nature in the Christian sphere of ideas. Yet the notion of moral solidarity is by no means confined to this sphere, and on the other hand many Christian sects have denied it. It corresponds to the view that the very *omission* of the act of love is sinful — for it is caused by excessive sensuous limitation to certain objects — and that the rise or decline of moral values is not bound to their visible manifestations which become part of historical tradition. Clearly these two premises are not given in the conception of modern humanitarian love.[9] Moreover, when a morality springs from those who are certain of their value, who accept and affirm their deepest self and being, who live in the fullness of their wealth, it always tends to *extend* "responsibility" as far as possible beyond the limits of the individual person — especially to all those whose lives are in some way dependent on this person's life. Conversely, it is a sign of "slave morality" — in Nietzsche's term — to *limit* responsibility as much as possible, to reject all guilt for the acts of "others," and at the same time to "accept no presents" in this respect.[10] The idea of moral solidarity, which has become almost incomprehensible to modern man, presupposes (as it were) an *inner capitalization* of moral values in the "kingdom of God" in whose result *all* individuals share and can share again and again.[11] The attitude underlying this notion is one of horror at the very *appearance* of evil, no matter who brings it about, and delight in the appearance of the good. The destiny of *all* mankind, indeed of all spiritual persons, is always felt to be implicated in both phenomena. "Here all stand for one and one for all."[12]

As long as a group is interested in the realization of the highest objective values, the question *who* realizes them will be of secondary importance, although each individual will be intent on doing it. Matters change when this attitude moves into the background — a natural corollary of a subjectivization of values[13] as it is taught by most modern philosophers. The tendency to reject responsibility for the guilt of others naturally follows from this change in experiencing values. Moreover, it follows from an attitude of basic *distrust* of the other person's moral value. If one thinks and feels that other people, everything else being equal, "have evil designs," one will naturally refuse responsibility for their acts.[14]

It is essential to note that modern morality is in every respect founded on *distrust* of men, particularly of their moral values. The merchant's fear of being cheated by his competitor has become the basic category of the very perception of others. It is this "distrust," so closely akin to *ressentiment,* which has brought about modern moral individualism and the denial of the principle of solidarity — attitudes that seem perfectly "self-evident" nowadays.

The second principle of modern morality, a consequence of the exclusive appreciation of what is self-acquired, is the doctrine of the *moral equality* of all men. Supposedly there are no value distinctions between men *independently* of the individual's own moral activity — neither before God and his grace, nor through original differences in the "potentialities" of individuals, races, nations, or even mankind as a whole as against the animal kingdom, nor through heredity or tradition. Both Greek antiquity and Christianity recognize such distinctions: the former in the Greco-Roman doctrine of the "natural institution" of slavery, the latter in the doctrines of the moral significance of grace and of the differences in natural moral gifts.

But the modern doctrine of equality as a whole — whether it pretends to be a statement of fact, a moral "postulate," or both — is obviously an achievement of *ressentiment*.[15] The postulate of equality — be it moral, social, political, ecclesiastical equality or equality of property — seems harmless, but who does not detect behind it the desire to degrade the *superior* persons, those who represent a higher value, to the level of the low? Nobody demands equality if he feels he has the strength or grace to triumph in the interplay of forces, in any domain of value! Only he who is afraid of *losing* demands equality as a *general principle*. The postulate of equality always involves "selling short"! It is a law that men can only be equal in their *least* valuable characteristics. The notion of "equality" as such, as a purely rational idea, can never actuate the will, the desire, and the affects. But *ressentiment,* unable to acquiesce in the sight of the higher values, conceals its nature in the postulate of "equality." In reality it merely wants to decapitate the bearers of higher values, at whom it takes offence![16]

When the tenet of the original equality of spiritual gifts is taken as a statement of fact, it means that all existing inequalities can be reduced to different quantities of *work* and experience or (if this is impossible) are founded on "unjust" artificial institutions which the pathos of our era now does its best to destroy.

## 2. THE SUBJECTIVIZATION OF VALUES

All modern theories of value share the premise that values as such, and moral values in particular, are only *subjective* phenomena in man's mind which have no independent meaning and existence. Values, according to this view, are but the projections of our desires and feelings. "What is desired is good, what is abhorred is bad." Reality as such, without human desires and emotions, is supposed to be entirely value-free.[17]

This basic modern view leads to one of two conclusions, both of which have become points of departure of modern morality. It entails either a justification of complete anarchy in questions of moral judgment, so that nothing at all seems "certain" in this respect, or the assumption of a substitute for true objectivity of value, a presumedly generally valid "generic consciousness" which asserts its power over the individual through an imperious "thou shalt." In the second case, the *general* recognition of "recognizability" of an act and desire as "good" is supposed to compensate for the non-existent *objectivity* of the value.

At the origin of this notion as well, *ressentiment* was the moving force. The *ressentiment*-laden man, who in his insufficiency is oppressed, tormented, and frightened by the negative judgment on his existence which flows from an *objective* hierarchy of values — and who is secretly aware of the arbitrary or distorted character of his own valuations[18] — "transvalues" the idea of value itself by *denying* the existence of such an objective hierarchy. In verbal formulation, the tendency of this inner movement would look as follows: "Your values (i.e., the values of those who are justified and 'good' according to the objective value hierarchy) are not 'more,' not 'better' than our values (which we ourselves feel to be 'arbitrary' and 'subjective'). Down with them! '*All*' values are 'subjective'!" It is the process we observe so often: the man of *ressentiment began* with the natural intention of willing "the good," and (uncorrupted as yet by certain delusions) he considers it "at first" as objective, eternal, and independent of human insight and desire. But as his efforts are less and less successful and as his envy and hatred for those who are objectively "good" grows by necessity, he increasingly tends to devaluate the idea of "goodness" *itself* by degrading it to the mere X of his *factual desire* and condition. A positive will of reform manifests itself differently: instead of the *hitherto accepted* content of objective goodness, the reformer may see and affirm *another* content that becomes the "only good" for him and to which he now devotes his life and activity. The man of *ressentiment,* however, wreaks vengeance on the *idea* whose test he cannot stand by pulling it down to the level of his factual condition. Thus his awareness of sin and nothingness explodes the beautiful structure of the world of values, debasing the idea for the sake of an illusory cure. "All values, after all, are 'only' relative and 'subjective' — they vary with the individual, with desire, race, people, etc."

But soon the need for binding forms of judgment will reappear. The man of *ressentiment* is a weakling; he cannot stand *alone* with his judgment. He is the absolute opposite of the type of man who realizes objective goodness against a whole world of resistance even when he is alone to see and feel it. Thus the *"generality"* or *"general validity"* of a judgment becomes his substitute for the true *objectivity* of value. He turns away from his personal quest for the good and seeks support in the question: What do you think? What do all people think? What is the "general" tendency of man as a species? Or what is the trend of "evolution," so that I may recognize it and place myself in its "current"? *All* collectively are supposed to see what no one alone can see and recognize: a positive insight is to result from the accumulation of zero insights! A thing that is never "good" in itself is supposed to become good simply because it was so yesterday, or because it is a direct descendant of yesterday's good!

Little children and slavish natures have the habit of excusing their acts by asking: "Have the others not done what I did?" According to *genuine* morality, companionship in badness makes it *worse,* for the badness of imitation and slavishness is added to the badness of the desired *content.* But here such companionship becomes a presumed "right" to make "good" what is bad! Thus the herds of *ressentiment*-laden men flock together more and more, thinking that their herd mentality is a substitute for the previously denied *"objective goodness."* Even in theory, the objectivity of the good is now replaced by a "generally valid law of human volition" (Kant) or, even worse, by an identification of "good" and "generic" volition.[19]

Already the philosophy of the Enlightenment has pushed this substitution of "generality" or "general validity" for "objectivity" to the utmost extreme. In all problems of value — whether they concern law, the state, religion, economy, science, or art — that which all men can produce and judge takes on the importance of an "ideal" by which we should measure the *concrete* and *positive* creations of civilization. The meaning of the expression "generally human" is endowed with the highest value. However, the psychological basis of this attitude is nothing but *hatred and negativism* against *every positive* form of life and civilization, which is always a courageous rise *above* what is merely "generally human" and must therefore come to naught when judged by this criterion.[20] If we take an object (and especially a value object) in the plain sense of true objectivism, general agreement in its acknowledgment is at best a *social criterion* for the social *right of affirming* its existence — it can never be a criterion for the *truth* of this affirmation, and even less for the essence of objectivity. Therefore the fact that *one* nation or *one* group, however small, is alone in understanding and acknowledging a domain of value can never be a meaningful argument against its genuineness and its reality. There are mathematical problems and theories that only a few people can as much as understand. The same can be true in the moral and religious sphere. Certain spiritual attitudes in religion, such as believing or divining — acts whose accomplishment may presuppose particular ways and forms of life which demand systematic exercise (asceticism) — can *very well* be subjective preconditions for experiencing certain domains of reality. People to whom these acts and ways of life are foreign are "blind" to those realities, and precisely that type of "human intelligence" which represents a "universally human capacity" is the least sufficient organ for apprehending them! Not the genuine notion of existence and objectivity, but only one which is already falsified, excludes this limitation.

Quite independently of its specific meaning and significance in positive religions, the concept of "revelation" has a place in the system of objectivism: it indicates that objective truths and values which presuppose a highly developed gift of cognition and feeling can be *communicated* to another group that has no organ for their original apprehension. This group must "believe" what others "see." In this formal sense, "revelation" is a *fundamental concept* of epistemology and of every genuine human civilization. It necessarily appears wherever *competence* in the knowledge of truths and values, and in the social distribution of such knowledge, is the decisive criterion — and not the question whether an affirmation corresponds to a "universal capacity."[21]

Matters are different when *ressentiment* falsifies the notion of objectivity, substituting "general validity" and universal recognizability! Then, of course, whatever is only limitedly "communicable," what cannot be communicated at all or only on the basis of certain ways of life — what is not "verifiable," and indeed whatever cannot be explained to the most stupid person, is necessarily taken to be "subjective imagination"! For this modern delusion, the national differences between moral and aesthetic values, between religious and legal systems are in themselves sufficient proof that values are not grounded in *things,* but only in "human, subjective, changing needs." This is in accordance with that fine criterion that places collective convention *above* "truth" and "goodness" and is but *one* of the logical formulations of the *ressentiment* directed against all that is unattainable to the common herd.

The elimination of "revelation" from the constitutive forms of cognition that exist independently of sensory experience and reason is an achievement of *ressentiment,* which wants to make "general human cognizability" the criterion of truth and existence.

### 3. THE ELEVATION OF THE VALUE OF UTILITY ABOVE THE VALUE OF LIFE

The chief manifestation of the *ressentiment* slave revolt in modern morality is the fact that the ultimate *material values themselves,* to which all values can be reduced — and not only the *men* who have to realize them in accordance with their class, work, and profession — are placed into a rank order that not only fails to correspond to their true place in the hierarchy of values, but actually *reverses* it.

This appears not only in the specifically moral judgments of our time, but also in its science and its theoretical world view.[22] The result is that modern morality can without contradiction appeal to contemporary "science." In fact, it is supported by the data and theory of this science and can even be "proved" by it, within the limits of this ideal of knowledge. But unfortunately the "ideal of knowledge" is itself based on *ressentiment* valuation. Thus a theory supports a practice which was itself the origin of this theory!

We begin by examining the moral-practical aspect of what is actually a uniform and concrete total process.

Among essential values there are two that have medium rank: the *value of utility* and the *vital value. It is evident that the latter is preferable to the former.*[23] We can also speak of the value of "preservation" and that of "expansion," the value of "adaptation" and that of "conquest," the value of the "tool" and that of the "organ."

This preference is determined by the *nature* of each value. The values of the first series are founded on those of the second in the sense that they can only be experienced if the others are given in some measure. Every value of utility is a value "for" a *living being.* Something is "useful" if it is a controllable cause for the realization of a good that is agreeable to the senses. But the feeling of pleasure is itself determined not only by the nature of a mind in general, but of a mind that acts through some specific form and organization of *life* which, taken as a *whole,* represents a certain vital *value.* This vital value cannot be reduced to the criterion of pleasure, since acts and things that tend to diminish vital values can also be "pleasurable."[24] One can easily imagine vital values without pleasure, but the reverse is impossible. It is no doubt evident that pleasurable things are preferable to unpleasant ones. But the value of *both* is itself determined by their capacity or incapacity of *strengthening vital* values. Therefore a pleasurable thing that obstructs life is bad. Thus the value of pleasurable things, independently of the degree of pleasure they afford, depends on the value of the living beings who feel them to be pleasurable. A thing that gives pleasure to a vitally valuable being is preferable to one that gives pleasure to a vitally less valuable being. Moreover, it is a characteristic of every kind of descending life that the things and acts it feels to be agreeable are those which advance the *decline* of life toward which it unconsciously tends. The perversion of desire and feeling, which leads the *"normally"* disagreeable things to appear agreeable, is a consequence of the feeling that life is declining. For this reason, the pleasure values — or the things and circumstances which are sources of pleasure, such as property — should not be equally distributed to all men according to "justice." Their distribution should be governed by the criterion that different men have different claims to those values, in accordance with their own vital value. Any tendency toward an "equal" distribution of the pleasure values would be "bad," for it would "unjustly" harm those who have greater vital value and therefore harm life *as such.* It would actuate an increasing perversion of sense experience. More and more things and acts that are essentially harmful to life would come to be considered as pleasurable.

Through its relation to pleasure, the value of "utility" is equally dependent on the value of *vitality.* This dependence is further enhanced by the fact that not every cause for pleasure is useful, but only that cause which can be controlled by volition. Only the *living being* can exercise this *control.* The measure in which a cause is *useful* for pleasure is partly determined by the degree to which it is subject to such control. Thus when the activity for the production of causes (means) of pleasure becomes subservient to these means, so that its kind and intensity is no longer dependent on the possibility of controlling the means (with a view to vitally valuable goals), then this activity itself becomes "bad." Then the whole system behind it is an expression of descending life. For it follows from the law of preference established above that every increase of causes for pleasure is harmful if these causes are no longer vitally controllable, and if the strength of controlling them is not the criterion of their distribution.

To sum up: Life "should" only produce useful things and enjoy pleasure in accordance with its rank in the scale of vital values and with its ability freely to control the useful things.

Modern morality, however, has subverted and reversed this intrinsically valid hierarchy of values not only in one respect, but in a whole series of relations.[25]


*Utility and Pleasure*

Nothing can meaningfully be called "useful" except as a means to pleasure. Pleasure is the basic value, utility the derived value. The enjoyment of pleasure is the meaning behind every utilitarian civilization — at least to the extent that this civilization produces useful things. Therefore the definitive value of such things depends among others on their owners' *capacity* of enjoying them. If the effort to produce them diminishes the capacity of enjoyment, it is not "worth the trouble." It is true that enjoyment can and should be subordinated to higher values, such as vital values, spiritual values of culture, "sacredness." But subordinating it to utility is an absurdity, for this is a subordination of the end to the means.[26]

Nevertheless it has become a rule of modern morality that useful work is better than the enjoyment of pleasure.

This is an example of a specifically *modern* type of asceticism, equally foreign to antiquity and to the Middle Ages. Its mainspring is an essential component of the inner forces which led to the formation of modern capitalism.[27] In a sense, this form of asceticism is the exact opposite of evangelical "asceticism," which aimed at *intensifying* the vital functions and with them the capacity of enjoying pleasure.

It is a characteristic of modern asceticism that the enjoyment of pleasure, to which all utility should be referred, undergoes a continual shift — until at last it is pleasure which is subordinated to utility. Here again, the propelling motive of the hard-working modern utilitarian is *ressentiment* against a superior capacity and art of enjoyment, hatred and envy of a richer life that can enjoy pleasure more fully. Thus pleasure and its enjoyment become "evils" as compared with utility, which in reality has no value except as a means to pleasure. An infinitely complex mechanism for the production of pleasurable objects is created and maintained by unceasing toil — but *without* any reference to the ultimate enjoyment of these objects. Psychologically, this unbridled impulse to work for utility's sake springs from a diminished capacity of enjoyment. Moreover, it progressively consumes whatever such capacity may be left. The result is that those who put in *the greatest amount* of useful work, thus taking possession of the external means for enjoyment, are *least* capable of using them. Conversely, the more vital groups, unable to compete with the others' work precisely because of their desire for enjoyment, increasingly lack the means of putting this desire into practice. Therefore the endless accumulation of pleasurable objects produced by modern civilization tends to benefit *nobody*. We ask: what is the use of the endless production of such objects if the type of man who consumes himself in producing them, and who owns them, is fundamentally incapable of enjoying them — while the man who could enjoy these objects is deprived of them?

Pleasurable things are incessantly being produced with vehemence, and *growing* energy and seriousness (and even sacrifice of vitality) are devoted to that task. But the enjoyment of these toilsomely produced things is rejected as "bad" with equal vehemence. Thus modern civilization acquires a specifically "comical" and "grotesque" aspect.

Formerly, the ideal of asceticism was to attain maximum *enjoyment* of pleasure with a minimum of *agreeable* and especially *useful objects.* Its aim was to enhance man's ability of drawing pleasure even from the simplest and most accessible things, such as nature. This indeed was one effect of the commandments of voluntary poverty, obedience, chastity, contemplation of things worldly and divine. Thus a small amount of "pleasure mechanisms" produced *degrees* of enjoyment for which the weaker life requires greater quantities of such mechanisms. The useful object was nothing but a means for enjoyment, and the man most capable of enjoyment was he who needed the *minimum* amount of agreeable things. Pre-modern asceticism enhanced the capacity for enjoyment and therefore intensified life, whether such was its direct aim or not.[28]

Modern asceticism, however, developed an ideal whose ethical core is the exact *opposite:* the *"ideal" of a minimum of enjoyment with a maximum amount of pleasant and useful things!* And indeed we can see that wherever work has assumed the hugest dimensions (as in Berlin and the large Northern German cities in general),[29] the capacity and art of enjoyment has reached the lowest degree imaginable. The abundance of agreeable stimuli here literally deadens the function of enjoyment and its cultivation. The surroundings become ever more glaring, merry, noisy, and stimulating — but men's minds become increasingly joyless. Extremely merry things, viewed by extremely sad people who do not know what to do with them: that is the "meaning" of our metropolitan "culture" of entertainment.

## On Utility Value and Vital Value in Particular

But the *most profound* perversion of the hierarchy of values is the *subordination of vital values to utility values,* which gains force as modern morality develops. Since the victory of the industrial and commercial spirit over the military and theological-metaphysical spirit, this principle has been penetrating ever more deeply, affecting the most concrete value judgments. Putting it briefly, we can say that the *"noble"* is being subordinated to the *"useful"* — "noble" standing for those qualities that constitute the value of life in living organisms. First the rise of the bourgeoisie since the 13th century, then the emancipation of the Third Estate in the French Revolution and in the political-democratic movement led to the establishment of a new structure of society. This new social structure is the *external* political-economic expression of the shift in values caused by the *ressentiment* which accumulated during the period when all life was organized along predominantly authoritative lines. This *ressentiment* exploded, its values spread and were victorious. As the merchants and representatives of industry came to dominate, especially in the Western countries, *their* judgments, tastes, and inclinations became the selective determinants of cultural production even in its intellectual and spiritual aspects. Their symbols and conceptions of the ultimate nature of things, which were necessary results of their activity, came to replace the older religious symbols, and everywhere *their* type of valuation became the criterion of "morality" as such.[30]

*Ressentiment* is an essential cause of this great process as well.

The reversion of values appears above all in the fact that the merchant's and the industrialist's professional values, the qualities that enable this particular type of man to succeed and do business, are set up as *generally valid* (indeed the "highest") *moral values*. Cleverness, quick adaptability, a calculating mind, a desire for "security" and for unhampered communication in all directions (and the qualities that are fit to bring about these conditions), a sense for the "calculability" of all circumstances, a disposition for steadiness in work and industriousness, economy and accuracy in concluding and observing agreements: these are the cardinal virtues now. They are set above courage, bravery, readiness to sacrifice, daring, high-mindedness, vitality, desire for conquest, indifference to material goods, patriotism, loyalty to one's family, tribe, and sovereign, power to rule and reign, humility, etc. But the transformation of concepts is even more profound when they bear the same *name*.[31] This we demonstrated for the "love of mankind." But terms like "justice," "self-control," "loyalty," "veracity," "economy," etc. also take on a *new* meaning. According to the older notion, *justice* prevailed only when the same thing happened to *equals,* and only *insofar* as they were equal, in accordance with the old Germanic tenets "suum cuique" and "si duo idem faciunt, non est idem." Therefore no one can justly be tried except by his equals. But the modern concept of justice, which coincides with the new idea of the factual "equality of all men," implies that all legislation for one particular group is *ipso facto* an instance of "unjust discrimination." It demands equal treatment for all, an equal distribution of profits and losses, goods and evils among *all* men and groups under the same external circumstances — without reference to the differences in their natures and talents.[32] Thus the principle that only equals should judge equals naturally disappears more and more, even in legal theory and practice.

— Originally, *"self-control"* meant primarily the sovereignty of the spiritual person over the chaos of sensuous impulses, the knightly will to dominate one's "appetites," the proud feeling — ruled by humility before and "in" God — that one is strong enough to tame them, regardless of whether the consequences are good or bad from the point of view of personal utility. But now self-control becomes a mere means to run one's business successfully with the aid of "soberness," "solidity," and "moderation" — if possible to the point of prevailing over one's competitor. When there is no such goal, self-control is not considered as a positive value.

— *"Loyalty"* used to be the natural continuity and permanence of a disposition of love and confidence. The requirement of binding "promises," of "agreements" to be concluded, was felt to be an *insult,* since it questioned this natural continuity and asked for an *artificial* guarantee. Yet now, "loyalty" is nothing but a disposition to adhere to such promises and agreements in practice.

— *"Veracity"* was once chiefly the courage of self-affirmation, the opposite of submissiveness to valuations and interests not one's own — the liar always submits to them, at least momentarily. Now "veracity" more and more comes to mean that one should not do or think anything that could not be *said* as well before the forum of social morality and public opinion!

— *"Economy"* was originally prized as a minor expression of the tendency embodied in the evangelical ideal of "voluntary poverty" — i.e., the idea of sacrifice. Moreover, it was valued as a form of vital fitness (not a "virtue"!) for the *poor* and for them alone. Now, without reference to the idea of sacrifice and the evangelical ideal, "economy" is elevated to a "virtue" — and, decisively, the virtue of the *rich* — but in such a way that Christian pathos remained attached to the

word. Sombart sharply points this out in his discussion of
Alberti: "That was the new, unheard-of thing: that one had
the means and *still* economized! *The idea of economy appeared
in the world!* Economy not by necessity, but by choice — not
as a need, but as a virtue. The *thrifty* manager becomes the
ideal even of the rich to the degree they had become 'bourgeois.'[33]

Justice, self-control, loyalty, veracity, and economy are only some
examples. An analogous transformation occurs in terms designating
all kinds of abilities. Even when the valuable qualities seem to remain
the same, something entirely new is *meant* by the old words.

The hierarchy of goods is transformed in a similar way.

Now life itself — the sheer *existence* of an individual, a race, a nation — must be justified by its *usefulness* for a *wider* community. It is
not enough if this life in itself contains higher values than usefulness
can represent — its existence must be "earned." The right to live and
exist, which the older morality included among the "natural rights," is
denied both in theory and in practice. On the contrary: if a man cannot adapt himself to the mechanism of the utilitarian civilization and
the human activity it happens to require at the moment, he *"should"*
be destroyed, no matter how great his vital values may be. According
to the earlier notion, life in its aimless *activity,* its mere "respiration"
and its characteristic inner processes, represents an intrinsic fullness of
value; all useful actions are destined to *serve* it, and all mechanisms are
only means to aid its *freer* development. Life is, as it were, the *innate
lord and master of the inanimate world,* it does *not* owe its value to the
benefits derived from its adaptation to the inanimate world and to
its capacity for being useful. But this original view is replaced by the
feeling that the pure expression of life is only ballast and evil luxury
— a kind of "atavistic survival" of forms of behavior and action that
were useful long ago.

In accordance with this basic idea, the ability to treat life as an
intrinsic value disappears in theory and practice. Therefore we also lose
all understanding for a *technique of life* — be it a technique of propagation, be it a social and individual technique for the intensification of
vital forces. Most older civilizations had such techniques: the castes

for the selection of the best and for the advancement of physical, intellectual, and moral hereditary values; the fixed, almost automatic systems for the distribution of cultural goods; the many forms of asceticism, exercise, contest, knightly tournament; India's caste system and asceticism; the estate system, races, games, and the Gymnasium of ancient Greece; the estate system, asceticism, knightly games and tournaments of the Middle Ages; the training of a Japanese Samurai; the ancient Chinese rank order and system of education — all these embody the same idea: that a dead mechanical technique stands below a vital technique, that life and the abundance of its forces deserves to be developed for its own sake — without reference to professional usefulness! Modern civilization is alone in lacking such a vital technique — and not only in practice: it has lost its pure idea![34] Even the last remnants of a social hierarchy — as a meaningful selection of the best and an image of the aristocracy that pervades all living nature — are cast overboard, and society is atomized in order to free the forces required for doing better business. The "estate" — a concept in which noble blood and tradition determine the unity of the group — is replaced by the mere "class," a group unified by property, certain external customs ruled by fashion, and "culture." Bodily training in all its forms is nothing but "recreation" from work or the gathering of strength for renewed useful labor — it is never valuable *in itself* as a pure play of vital forces. There is no longer the slightest understanding for the exercise of vital functions for the sake of life (nor indeed for the exercise of thought for the sake of thought, as in the dialectics of the ancients) — everything is done for the sake of work. Vital and spiritual asceticism, the distribution of the traditional means of education and the acquired spiritual treasures according to the different potentialities of different groups — all this has become incomprehensible. Mechanical chance governs everything. "True seriousness" pertains to business and work alone, and all the rest is only "fun." Even modern "sports" are nothing but recreation from work, and by no means a manifestation of free vitality at whose service work itself should be.[35]

Biological theory finds "facts and reasons" to justify this primary variation of the hierarchy of values. At the core of the new world view which has been developing since Descartes, "life" itself is no longer an *original phenomenon,* but merely a complex of mechanical and mental processes. The mechanistic view of life sees the living being itself as a "machine," its "organization" as a sum of useful tools which differ only in degree from artificially produced tools. If this were true, then naturally life could have no independent *value* apart from the combined utility values of these "organs." The idea of an independent technique of life, fundamentally different from mechanical technique, would be equally meaningless. In fact such a technique of life would often require the development of abilities that run counter to an efficient machine technique. Furthermore, for modern biology it is almost self-evident that the expressions, movements, and actions of the living being, and the organs and nervous system serving them, are only developed and propagated to the degree that they are useful for the preservation of the bodily machine. An unprejudiced look at the facts will show that there are "trial movements" from which the successful useful movements are only later developed by selection;[36] expressive movements[37] which simply "express" the plenitude or poverty of life, without objective "goals"; "instinctive movements" which serve the species over and above the preservation of the individual; playful expressions of pure vitality. Yet biological theory reduces them all to the criterion of utility. It explains these movements by assuming either that they were once useful and have now lost this character, or that their usefulness is not yet dear to science, or that they represent embryonic beginnings of such movements.

These biological views, whose fundamental falsity cannot be demonstrated here, are also applied to the problem of the origin of *civilization* and *culture*. Here again, considerations of utility are supposed to have brought about the formation of tools, science, the origin of language, and the development of art and religion.[38]

Thus the practice of life is closely connected with theory. The theory seems to justify the practice, but in reality it is determined by the same shift in values.

This view of life has more or less conquered the civilized world and has come to be dominant chiefly in England. It is not, as is mistakenly assumed, the source of utilitarian and mechanistic philosophy since Bacon, but rather a demonstrable descendant of this philosophy. It has four *basic characteristics:*

1. It considers every vital totality (individual, organ, kind, species, etc.) as a *sum of parts* whose interaction engenders the process of life. Thus the individual is a "system of cells."

2. It views the "organ" by analogy with the *"tool"* made of dead matter. Only such a tool is supposed to be originally "useful." Thus the technical creation of tools is considered to be an "immediate continuation" of the organ-forming process (Herbert Spencer is typical here).

3. It reduces all "phenomena of growth and development" to the impulse of "preservation," so that they become epiphenomena of preservation processes or "adaptations to the environment." The individual's tendencies to sacrifice himself for his contemporaries or for the next generation are held to be reducible to his urge of preserving himself or the greatest number of individuals. In other words: the processes of propagation are taken as individual activities, and the forces and substances required for these processes are seen as parts (or partial functions) of the individuals and individual functions.

4. The physical organism is not viewed as the locus and bearer of vital phenomena which are produced by an independent uniform force. No: "life" as such is only a composed quality, inherent in the combination of forces and substances that make up the organism. Life disappears when this combination is dissolved. Hence the gross references to a so-called "living substance."

These principles account for the valuation which may be considered the ruling *ethos of industrialism:* the exaltation of utility values and instrumental values over vital and organic values. This rule of preference is maintained even in the smallest concrete judgments. It is rooted in the *ressentiment* of the vitally unfit against the fit, of those who are partially dead against the living! The common root of all these principles is everywhere the same: the vital process is viewed by analogy with *images* and *categories* drawn from the way in which man — as a fixed type that has ceased to develop — belabors dead matter. The structure of a utilitarian civilization is thus projected into the realm of natural life.[39] This, however, is merely a variety of "anthropomorphism": the anthropomorphism of the specifically human "intellect." But in a certain section of its categories and forms of thinking, the "intellect" is itself only one of the vital functions, characteristic of a species that has become *stable*. The intellect can comprehend the universe only as a "mechanical" universe, and this mechanical universe is then made the basic "milieu" of universal life, the lock for this key. The differences between organisms are not seen as different factors *forming* the milieu, but as different adaptations to the (human) surroundings, varying only in degree. The various forms of consciousness (of the plant, the animal, and man), which differ essentially from each other, are interpreted as mere stages in the development toward the human "intellect." The explanation of life in terms of mechanical principles is only the ultimate scientific expression of this procedure. For these principles do not embody the pure intellect or the essence of "reason," but rather the intellect and reason are here considered as useful in the creation of tools.[40] Thus all philosophical rationalism — which mistakes the mechanical principles for expressions of pure reason and thinks that their correlate, the universe reduced to a mechanism, is the "world" which surrounds all living beings — turns out to be "anthropomorphism." In fact, the mechanical universe is nothing but the purest and most perfect expression of those principles of selection with whose aid *man* reduces all phenomena to the unity of his milieu. It is the expression of generic predilection for solid movable objects, the real *a priori* of "man." In reality, the mechanical universe is only a small part (u) of the universe (u'). The latter is the correlate of the whole world of living beings and is in its turn only a small section of the Universe (U), the correlate of the universal spiritual personality. Thus u is nothing more than the "world of human labor."[41]

Here it is our task to examine the substance of the principles enunciated above, but only with a view to their impact on valuation, and to show that *ressentiment* is the psychological source of their falsity.

About 1: *the living being as a sum of parts.*

If this notion were correct, it would follow that the existing units of life (individual, organ, tissue, cell, but also species, variety, etc. — in other words: both intra-individual and supra-individual units) are nothing but fortuitous aggregates. Their unity would be due to physical and chemical forces, and apart from that it would be a mere *subjective* aggregation in consciousness. To make *one* being of this combination of cells, we must have recourse to the conscious "ego." The resulting picture is that of a gigantic, strictly continuous and coherent system of movements, reaching from my brain and lungs up to the sun and the fixed stars. We have organic units when intelligent egos ("res cogitantes") use certain partial systems of these movements. This is the only determination of organic unity, and when there is no such ego, then we have nothing but complicated dynamic processes into which we, as subjective observers, falsely project emotional experiences! We are nothing but thinking points in an immense mechanical process!

We see that everything living and vital is eliminated from this strange picture. This world is an accumulation of logicians standing in a huge engine-room — bloodless, emotionless, without love or hatred.

It is the gigantic symbol, the caricature of modern man! Since all these units are only sums of parts, the value of the whole depends on the added values of the parts. A healthy man is he who has the maximum number of healthy cells, a healthy nation is one which has the maximum number of healthy citizens, etc. One will speak of progress when the goal of all activity is the existence and survival of the maximum number of life units.

Applied to man, this principle leads straightway to *democratism.* By democratism[42] I mean the principle that the preservation of a maximum *number* of human beings is the goal of all positively valuable activity. Above all, it excludes a *primary solidarity* between the different parts of mankind, which would mean that the fortunes of these parts concern the *whole* and that different individuals, nations, and races are solidary with the whole to *different* degrees. For such "solidarity" would presuppose that the unity of life is a primary quality which precedes the parts and inheres in them, though with varying intensity.

Thus the principle of summation is in contradiction with the principle of solidarity.[43] Both in idea and feeling, it entails a fundamentally different relation between the individual and the community. Under the sway of the principle of solidarity, everyone knows and feels that the community as a *whole* is inherent in him — he feels that his blood is the blood which circulates in the community, that his values are part of the values which permeate the community. Here all values are *based* on solidarity of feeling and willing. The individual is the community's organ and at the same time its representative; its honor is his honor. This material inherence in the community is now replaced by the notion that the community is only the product of the *interaction* between the individuals. The communal values are supposedly created by adding up the values invested in the individuals. The individual values circulate merely through conscious communication and instruction, or by conscious recognition and "agreement." To put it more simply: the "community" and its structure is replaced by "society," in which men are arbitrarily and artificially united by promise and contract.[44]

In fact, "society" is not the inclusive concept, designating all the "communities" which are united by blood, tradition, and history. On the contrary, it is only the *remnant,* the *rubbish* left by the inner *decomposition* of communities. Whenever the unity of communal life can no longer prevail, whenever it becomes unable to assimilate the individuals and develop them into its living organs, we get a "society" — a unity based on mere contractual agreement. When the "contract" and its validity ceases to exist, the result is the completely unorganized "mass," unified by nothing more than momentary sensory stimuli and mutual contagion. Modern morality is essentially a *"societal morality,"* and most of its theories are built on this basic notion. Thus the principle that each man's responsibility, guilt, and merit is limited to himself and his own actions — the negation of all primary *"co-responsibility."* We should add all "contractual theories," and theories such as the following: that the state, language, and custom are inventions; that all insight into other people's psychology is derived from conclusions by analogy with one's own experiences; that sympathy is subordinate and reducible to the impulse for self-preservation — and many other views.

Here again, the feelings and ideas of those elements the old "community" had cast aside (its pariahs) have determined the general image of man and his associations.[45] Even marriage and the family, whose relation to all other forms of community is that of microcosm to macrocosm and in which all elements of communal life are pre-formed and given in reduced proportions, were artificially more and more degraded to a matter of civil contract.

Wherever a "community" existed, we find that the *fundamental forms* of communal life were endowed with a value far *superior* to all individual interests, to all subjective opinions and intentions. Every violation of these "forms" led to punishment or proscription, irrespective of the individual's subjective intention and without any regard to his happiness or suffering. Thus marriage, whatever its empirical forms may be, is considered as an objectively holy "bond" which needs no justification before the spouses' happiness or misery, before their mutual intentions and feelings. It is a sanctified *form* through which the generations pass, not an instrument of individual pleasure and happiness. In ecclesiastical language, it is a "sacrament." Wherever there is a real community, the *forms* of life have an intrinsic value on which individual interests, joys, and sufferings have no bearing. This valuation disappears with the rise of "society"! Modern philosophy since Descartes declares all "forms" in nature to be mere syntheses in consciousness, thus denying their objective reality. In the same way, it makes the value of "communal forms" dependent on their furtherance of the *sum total* of individual happiness. Therefore these forms are always accessible to "reform," and instead of *respecting* them, one feels free to change them *arbitrarily.*

Another consequence of this basic attitude is the predominance of the principle of majority in politics and the state. In the communities, the will of the *whole* is manifested and revealed in the will of those who are the "noblest" by birth and tradition. Now, however, the will of the majority supposedly constitutes the will of the state.

All this shows the *victory of ressentiment in morality.* No one who is conscious of representing a value in which he is superior to the others will wish to be considered as "one and only one" (as Bentham, a classic of democracy, demands). Such a postulate can only be established by those who feel that they are worthless and who want to pull the others down to their level. Even if a man is *nothing* at all, he is still "one"!

About 2: *organ and tool.*

If the organism is a complicated machine-like mechanism, its organs can and should be considered as tools that do not differ in kind, but only in degree of complication from the artificial tools which man fabricates for his use. According to this view, a hand does not differ in essence from a knife or an ax. One can go so far as to say that the tool is only an "extension and amplification" of the natural organism, and that it realizes values of the same kind, nature, and quality as the development of the organism. The result as well is then the same: "adaptation to the surroundings"! This is the leading idea of Spencer's biology and sociology.[46]

But it is easy to see that an *image* is here mistaken for the *thing itself,* regardless of the question whether the organs develop with the aid of a selective, organizing intelligence conscious of its aims or by mere mechanical processes. In both cases the organ is conceived as a totality composed of spatially well-determined parts, and in both cases it is viewed as a mere means for "adapting" the organism to a supposedly constant milieu, closed in itself — the milieu of dead nature given in physics and chemistry. Neither of the two premises applies to the "organ."

The formation, growth, regeneration, etc. of an organ does not take place in the same way as we would go about it if we had the (insoluble) task of making one. We should not superimpose our method of understanding, which is adapted to dead matter, on the factual process of the genesis of life: that would be "anthropomorphism," applied to life and to man as a part of living nature.[47] The formation of organs is not an aggregation of parts of a spatially and qualitatively determined variety of substances. It depends on the formative activity of an agent belonging to a non-spatial multiplicity, which extends its action into space and completely penetrates the substances (regardless of their chemical and physical determination) without violating the principle of energy, but running counter to the course of the principle of entropy.[48] This cannot be demonstrated here. At any rate the formation of organs can only be understood if we assume that the *whole* unitary living being is active in each organ and that — in accordance with Kant's correct definition of the nature of the organism — the parts are not only there for the whole, but "the whole for the parts" as well. Furthermore, it is the most important principle of the formation of organs that *every* spatially determined part of the germ *can* develop into *any one* of the organs that make up the finished organism — subject to the limitations which the organs already formed impose on the uniform vital activity and its directions.[49] According to this biological principle, the formation of organs is *essentially* different from the formation of tools, which takes place and is "worth while" only when the vital agent is no longer able to create new organs

— i.e., when a species has become fixed and relatively unfit for purely vital development.

Moreover, the formation of organs is not an "adaptation" to a given dead natural milieu. The same process which forms the organ also determines the character and structure of the "milieu" or "nature" to which a species tries to adapt by means of tools.[50] The natural milieu to which man has adapted through tools and through his whole technical civilization is not a mere "datum" to which his vital activity must passively adapt itself. It has been *selected* from an abundance of phenomena by the course and direction of this vital activity. These phenomena in themselves do not have structure, but rather this structure is determined by the basic forms of man's intellect and perception. Bergson already revealed the fundamental error of mechanical biology: it tries to comprehend and explain vital phenomena by applying concepts and forms of perception that are proper to an "intellect" which has itself originated as *an instrument* of the specifically *human* vital activity and is completely dependent on its tendencies.[51]

In reality, the vital activity of the different species develops incessantly in its form and direction, *thrusting out* again and again into an infinite universe which flows around "nature" (i.e., the totality of phenomena defined by space, time, and mechanical causality) as the things we "divine" surround the horizon of our eye — like the sailor and explorer who sails out courageously into maritime regions never yet mapped by geographers. "Adaptation" by means of tools occurs and is meaningful only when the vital activity *stagnates* and can *no longer extend* the milieu by the formation of new organs. But the theory in question, inspired as it is by the *ressentiment* of the relatively dead against the living, wants to confine life within *limits* which it has itself set up in the course of its development. The formation of organs is interpreted as an "adaptation" to a "milieu" which is actually the result of a more or less permanent *stagnation* of the vital activity and of the formation of organs. The "milieu" to which we adapt our tools is in fact nothing but that corner which our vital organism has selected in the universe. It is by no means a totality which contains us as well as all other living beings and to which we have all "adapted" ourselves.

Guided by *ressentiment,* the modern world view reverses the true state of affairs. It "sells short," as all thinking geared to declining life, and seeks to understand the living by analogy with the dead. It interprets life as such as an accident in a universal mechanical process, the living organism as a fortuitous adaptation to a fixed dead milieu. The eye is explained by analogy with spectacles, the hand by analogy with the spade, the organ by analogy with the tool! No wonder that the mechanical civilization — which is always the result of a relative *stagnation* in vital activity and therefore a *surrogate* for the formation of organs — is mistaken for the triumph, continuation, and extension of vital activity. Thus the infinite "progress" of mechanical civilization becomes the true "goal" of all vital activity, and the infinite development of the calculating intellect is made the "meaning" of life.

This basic view on the relation between organ and tool naturally entails that the specific utility value of the tool is placed above both the "vital value" and the "cultural value."[52] In fact, in the last analysis this shift of values is the *source* rather than the consequence of this mistaken world view. Everything else being equal, it is the vitally inferior, relatively stagnant man — he who "got the worst of it" — who places the tool above the vital values he lacks! The near-sighted man will praise his eyeglasses, the lame man his stick, the bad mountain climber will extol the rope and climbing irons which the better one holds for him with his arms. We do not mean to imply that man should create no tools and that civilization as such was a "blunder" — that would be abominable nonsense. Man, as the biologically *most stable* species, must create civilizations, and he should do so — provided that the subordinate forces, and the forces of dead nature, are employed in order to relieve nobler forces. But he should remain within these *limits,* i.e., the tool should *serve* life and its expansion. The positive valuation of tools is not due to *ressentiment* — only the assumption that tools are as valuable as organs!

With the development of modern civilization, *nature* (which man had tried to reduce to a mechanism for the purpose of ruling it) and *objects* have become *man's lord and master,* and *the machine* has come to dominate *life.* The "objects" have progressively grown in vigor and intelligence, in size and beauty — while man, who created them, has more and more become a cog in his own machine. Perhaps there is no point on which there is more general agreement among sensible and right-minded contemporaries.

But it is not sufficiently clear that this generally acknowledged fact is due to a fundamental *subversion of values*. *Its source is ressentiment,* the victory of the value judgments of those who are vitally inferior, of the lowest, the pariahs of the human race! The entire mechanistic world view, to the degree that it lays claim to metaphysical truth, is only the immense intellectual *symbol* of the slave revolt in morality.[53] The rule of life over matter has weakened; the spirit (and the will above all) has lost much of its mastery over the automatism of life: that is the ultimate explanation for the expansion and development of the mechanistic world view, and of the corresponding values which created it.[54]

Once we have recognized this view on the relation between tool and organ to be mistaken, we will understand a whole series of modern phenomena which are based on this premise.

In the first place, there are the negative consequences of one-sided *industrialism.* If we believe that the "tool civilization" continues the formation of organs, then we are bound to desire the infinite development of industrialism, though it harms life in many ways. Let us mention woman and child labor, the disintegration of the family, the growth of big cities with their unhealthy living conditions, the harmful effects of poisons connected with technical processes, the specialization of all activity in the service of the machine until human beings become cogs, the growing dependence of marriage and procreation on money and property instead of vital qualities,[55] the dissolution of the national units. All these will be considered as more or less "passing ills" which will disappear with the still further development of industrialism. This is the justification of industrialism advanced by Herbert Spencer with strict and admirable consistency.

How differently do things look when this basic error is abandoned! Then the further development of industrialism is not unconditionally valuable, but only if it inflicts no permanent damage on vital values. Then we must say, for example: preserving the health of the race as a whole — and of the groups within it in proportion to their vital fitness and their vitally valuable, "noble" qualities and forces — is an *intrinsic value* and should be placed above useful achievements even if the industrial evolution is thus slowed down. Units such as the family and the nation need support and care, even if it demonstrably delays industrial progress and the expansion of civilization. A group within a people has no claim to being favored in the distribution of goods and honors because it produces a large quantity of useful consumer goods. It deserves preference according to the degree of its *historical political significance* for the construction and maintenance of a *vitally valuable* system of social hierarchy. Agriculture is intrinsically a more valuable activity than commerce and industry, and it deserves to be protected and furthered — if only because it entails a healthier way of living, which equally occupies all forces. It should be maintained and supported even if industrial progress yields greater economic *profit,* since it makes the national units *independent* of foreign countries. The same applies to the preservation of plant and animal life, and the woods, and to the protection of the landscape against the devastating tendencies of industrialism.

If we consider the transvaluation of the relation between tool and organ in its totality, we must conclude that the spirit of modern civilization does not constitute "progress" (as Spencer thought), but a *decline* in the evolution of mankind. It represents the rule of the weak over the strong, of the intelligent over the noble, the rule of mere quantity over quality. It is a phenomenon decadence, as is proved by the fact that everywhere it implies a *weakening of man's central, guiding forces* as against the anarchy of his automatic impulses. The mere means are developed and the goals are forgotten. And that precisely is decadence!

# NOTES

## Prefatory Remarks

*The German edition contains two systems of footnotes, separating Scheler's footnotes from those of the German editor, Maria Scheler. The two systems have been merged in this translation. Scheler's footnotes have all been translated, those of Maria Scheler (always between square brackets) for the major part. The very few references which have been left out are too exclusively destined for German readers. We added some footnotes of our own, which are marked by an asterisk (\*). Moreover, some bibliographical precisions have been supplied, both in the text and the footnotes. (Translator's Note)*

1. Cf. Karl Jaspers' often very pertinent remarks on the difference between causal connections *(Kausalzusammenhänge)* and understandable context *(Ver-ständniszusammenhänge)* in mental life, in his book *Allgemeine Psychopathologie* (Berlin, 1913).

2. On the peculiarity of these processes, cf. my book *Zur Phänomenologie und Theorie der Sympathiegefühle* (Halle, 1913), p. 7 ff. [Cf. the later extended version of this book, *Wesen und Formen der Sympathie* (1923; 4th ed. Frankfurt, 1948), part A, II.]

\* English translation of the latter: *The Nature of Sympathy*, tr. by Peter Heath (New Haven, Conn., 1954), part I, ch. II.

3.\* In the translation as well, the French term *"ressentiment"* has been maintained for the reasons which Scheler indicates: Nietzsche has made it a technical term, and it would be difficult to find an English word which adequately expresses the same nuances. The English word "resentment" is too specific. Its use has been avoided throughout the translation.

# I

## On the Phenomenology and Sociology of Ressentiment

1. Here is a list of Scheler's terms for the various emotions of this kind, with the English translations which have been used and consistently maintained: *Rache* (revenge), *Hass* (hatred), *Scheelsucht* (impulse to detract), *Hämischkeit* (spite), *Groll*

(rancor), *Zorn* (wrath), *Rachsucht* (vindictiveness, vengefulness). The term *Schaden-freude* (=joy at another's misfortune) has been left in German.

2. Steinmetz, in his interesting studies on the genealogy of revenge, assumes that "directed revenge" is preceded by "non-directed revenge." He argues that in the most primitive stages of civilization even animals (such as the nearest horse), trees, or inanimate objects are destroyed when an injury has been experienced. Steinmetz misinterprets the essential nature of revenge, which is always *directed,* in contrast with non-active affects such as wrath, anger, rage, etc. There are outbursts of rage even on a civilized level, for example, when someone whose anger has been aroused "cuts everything to pieces." These have nothing to do with revenge. Even if the examples given by Steinmetz should be cases of revenge, there are still several possibilities. The object destroyed may stand in a real or supposed property relation to the object of revenge or may be connected with it in a symbolic function which can be momentary and need not be permanent ("let this object stand for that person now"). Not only the destruction of books or the piercing of photographs, but also the crumbling of a piece of paper or a handkerchief may fall under this heading. Or revenge can be "without an object" in the sense that it may be directed against no *particular* object, but may comprise the whole region where the injury has been inflicted — a district, a city, or even the whole world in its "otherness." Such a case occurred only recently in the mass murders committed by the teacher Wagner. [Cf. Robert Gaupp's mono-graph Zur *Psychologie des Massenmordes: Hauptlehrer Wagner von Degerloch* (Berlin, 1914), to which the author's remark refers.] But revenge is "directed" even here. It has been wrongly assumed that vendetta is a secondary transference of the object of revenge to the offender's tribe or family members, caused by the awareness that the offender would suffer in sympathy with his stricken companion. But the true basis of vendetta is the view that the tribe or family is the real *perpetrator* and that the individual member is only its organ. It is as if I punish the man who cut off my hand by chopping off his foot. It seems, moreover, that revenge is in the last analysis not limited to injury or the diminution of one's value inflicted by another individual. It may also be caused by our own depreciation of ourselves or of others with whom we sympathize. This is the case when we say: "I could hit myself, I could tear my hair," etc. These phenomena have nothing to do with the act of repentance or the desire for atonement and expiation, which are spiritual acts rather than vital impulses and are exclusively connected with the realm of moral values. Cf. S. R. Steinmetz, *Eth-nologische Studien zur ersten Entwicklung der Strafe* (Leyden, 1894). Cf. also my essay on "Reue und Wiedergeburt" in *Vom Ewigen im Menschen.* [In the second edition of the essays and treatises *Vom Umsturz der Werte* (1919) — in this footnote as well as in some others — the work *Vom Ewigen im Menschen* is announced for as early as 1918. In fact it did not appear until 1921.]

3. J.-M. Guyau cites such examples in his book *Esquisse d'une morale sans obliga-tion ni sanction* (1885).

4. The enormous explosion of *ressentiment* in the French Revolution against the nobility and everything connected with its way of living, and indeed the very emergence of this *ressentiment,* would have been entirely inconceivable if (according to Werner Sombart's calculation in *Luxus und Kapitalismus,* Munich 1912, pp. 10-

24) more than 80% of the nobility itself had not been intermingled with bourgeois elements, who acquired names and titles by buying aristocratic estates. Besides, the nobility was racially weakened by money marriages. The *ressentiment* of the insurgents was sharpened by the new feeling that they were *equal* to the ruling class.

* There exists a mimeographed translation of Sombart's *Luxury and Capitalism* (New York, 1938), carried out under the auspices of the Works Progress Administration and the Department of Social Science of Columbia University, under the supervision of W. R. Dittmar.

5. Our present-day semi-parliamentarianism in the German Empire is conducive to the inner health of the people, since it serves as a discharge mechanism for accumulated *ressentiment*. But to the degree that the parliament is eliminated from active government, or at any rate from the function of selecting those men of the nation who have the strongest will and the most acute political intelligence, it attracts only a certain section of the men of *ressentiment:* those who accept that their votes of nonconfidence strengthen the position of the ministers rather than weaken it.

* Of course Scheler is referring to the German Empire prior to the First World War.

6. In the experience of envy, the mere fact that the other person possesses the coveted good is therefore felt to be a "deprivation." This is because our original mental attitude is characterized by an illusory *appropriation* of the good. The other person's suddenly discovered ownership of the good appears as a "deprivation," as a "force" which takes it away from us.

7. [This quotation is from *Maxims and Reflections,* "From the Elective Affinities," 45.]

8. Thus pride is always based on *lack* of this natural self-confidence.

9. [On *"arriviste"* and *"ressentiment,"* cf. Max Scheler, *Der Formalismus in der Ethik und die materiale Wertethik.* Cf. index of the 4th ed., 1954.]

10. [On this and what follows, cf. the essay "Der Bourgeois" in *Vom Umsturz der Werte.*]

11. Cf. Leopold von Ranke, *Über die Epochen der neueren Geschichte* (Munich, 1921), 1st lecture.

12. Cf. what follows.

13. Cf. *Formalismus,* part II. [On feeling, preferring, and loving as cognitive acts, and on the relation between value consciousness and acts of aspiration, cf. *Formalismus,* section I 3 and section V 2.] Cf. also my article "Ethik" in *Jahrbücher der Philosophie,* II. Jahrgang, Berlin 1914, ed. by Max Frischeisen-Köhler.

14. In an interesting study on "Christus und das Ressentiment" (supplement to Hambg. Korresp. of 28 Sept. 1913) A. Gustav Hübener, continuing the above, points out that in the view of the Christian Church even the devil has a glimmer of direct knowledge of the good. John Milton makes Satan acknowledge his principle as follows:

> "Farewell remorse: all good to me is lost,
> Evil be thou my good."

But still, heaven shines into his soul, so that he must cast furtive glances at it and stir up the infernal fire in his heart:

> "... the more I see
> Pleasures about me, so much more I feel
> Torment within me, as from the hateful siege
> Of contraries; all good to me becomes
> Bane, and in Heaven much worse would be my state."

15. Cf. my analysis of English "cant" in my book *Der Genius des Krieges und der deutsche Krieg* (Appendix, 3rd ed., 1917).

16. [Cf. the essay "Zum Sinn der Frauenbewegung" in *Vom Umsturz der Werte*.]

17. Cf. the views of the great 18th-century writers and philosophers on this matter, collected by Havelock Ellis in his book *The Evolution of Modesty* (Philadelphia, 1910). They all reduce modesty to "upbringing" and mistake it for "propriety." [Cf. the author's study on "Scham und Schamgefühl," published posthumously by the German editor in *Schriften aus dem Nachlass, Band 1: Zur Ethik und Erkenntnislehre*.]

18. The well-known inquiry of the "Verein für Sozialpolitik" shows how soon the qualified industrial worker is nowadays pushed down into the ranks of unqualified workers. [The title of the inquiry mentioned by the author is "Untersuchungen über Auslese und Anpassung (Berufswahl und Berufsschicksal) der Arbeiter in den verschiedenen Zweigen der Grossindustrie," Leipzig, 1911/12.]

19. Cf. *Luxus und Kapitalismus* (Berlin, 1912), p. 115.

20. Cf. Wilhelm Hasbach, *Die moderne Demokratie* (Jena, 1912).

21. All assertions in the book by Innocent III, *De contemptu mundi sive de miseria humanae conditionis,* are dictated by extreme priestly *ressentiment.*

22. Cf. *Genealogy of Morals,* part I, section 15.

23. Cf. the characterization of Tertullian by Johann Adam Möhler, *Patrologie* (Regensburg, 1840). He was bitter and gloomy by nature, and even the mild light of the Gospel could not brighten his gloom" (p. 703). Tertullian's conversion to Montanism (about 203 A.D.), after which he knew no limits in ridiculing and deriding the principles and customs of the Church, is merely a renewal of the act of apostasy, which had become the very structure of his vital reactions.

24. Already Sigwart *(Logik II)* rightly points out that Darwin's theory as well uses the basic Hegelian idea of the "creative importance of negation." According to Darwin, all evolution is essentially determined by the elimination of the useless within purely contingent variations of the species. Thus the impression of positive development and creativity which is conveyed by the sight of organized species is a mere epiphenomenon, behind which there is nothing but negation and elimination.

25. [In the first version of the present study (1912), before its extension, this passage followed.]

26. No other literature is as full of *ressentiment* as the young Russian literature. The books of Dostoevsky, Gogol, and Tolstoi teem with *ressentiment*-laden heroes.

This is a result of the long autocratic oppression of the people, with no parliament or freedom of press through which the affects caused by authority could find release.

27. We must exclude the type of anxiety which is genetically a fear that has lost its object. As all fear, it once had a definite object which has merely ceased to be clearly conscious. We must further except that type of anxiety which is primarily a mode of a person's vital feeling *(Lebensgefühl)* itself and which conversely *makes* him fear ever new objects, far beyond the danger they might hold. The former kind of anxiety can be easily removed, the latter almost never. The general pressure of anxiety which weighs on individuals and whole groups varies greatly in degree. It is highly important for the total behavior of the subjects concerned.

* The German terms used by Scheler are: *Furcht* (fear), *Angst* (anxiety), *Verängstigtheit* (anguish), *Eingeschüchtertheit* (intimidation).

28. Cf. the author's essay "Die Idole der Selbsterkenntnis" in *Vom Umsturz der Werte.*

29. Cf. the case of the captain of Köpenick. If one paid even slight attention, he certainly did not look like an officer. But the mere vague appearance of the "uniform," which he did not even wear according to regulations, was enough to make the mayor and the others obey all his orders.

30. We do not wish to decide here to what degree Paul, in his quotation, may be thinking of the salvation of him who blushes, who is awakened to new love by his shame and remorse.

31. Cf. William James, *Psychology* (New York, 1891).

32. Cf. the author's essay "Die Idole der Selbsterkenntnis" in *Vom Umsturz der Werte* and his treatise "Reue und Wiedergeburt" in *Vom Ewigen im Menschen.*

33. J.-M. Guyau, *Esquisse d'une morale sans obligation ni sanction.*

34. Cf. the author's book on *Formalismus,* where he attempts to prove this affirmation. [On *"ordre du coeur,"* "moral genius," and "historical apprehension of values," cf. *Formalismus,* section V 6; furthermore, the essay "Ordo Amoris," written about 1916, published posthumously in the previously mentioned *Nachlassband* (1933).]

35.Antonio's behavior toward Tasso (in Goethe's *Torquato Tasso)* is strongly colored by *ressentiment.* This is certainly a reflection of this Goethean experience of life.

36. [In the first version of the present study (1912), there follows an account of a pathological case.]

# II

## Ressentiment *and Moral Value Judgment*

1. The author's book *Formalismus* (especially part II) establishes the existence of an absolute ethics, which is here assumed without detailed proof, and interprets

the various kinds and stages in the historical variability of moral judgments. [Cf. especially section V 6. The terminology of the present essay differs somewhat from that in *Formalismus*, part II. There the author does not speak of an "absolute ethics," but of an absolute hierarchy of values which is the foundation of an *a priori* material ethics of value on a phenomenological basis. The most basic among the 5 principal layers of the variations of moral value judgment — i.e., the variation of feeling, preferring, and loving — is there designated as the variation of "ethos." "Ethics" is the philosophical systematization, carried out in judgments, of the values and hierarchical value relations which are given in these acts and functions. In *Formalismus*, the conceptual distinction of the variations of moral value judgments is more differentiated than in the present essay.]

2. The proof, which lies in the phenomenology of the stages of judging and willing, cannot be given here. It is contained in the above-mentioned book.

3. Cf. Wilhelm Worringer, *Abstraktion und Einfühlung* (Munich, 1919. In English: *Abstraction and Empathy*, tr. by M. Bullock, New York, 1953). His analysis is based on the research of Riegl.

# III

## *Christian Morality and* Ressentiment

1. Cf. *Genealogy of Morals*, part I, section 8.

2. It has been rightly said that the father's attitude toward his two sons is a blow against the ancient idea of justice.

3. The terminology is different only in the case of an erotic attachment of a man to a boy. Then the φιλόμενος is younger and less perfect, the ἐρασθής older and more perfect. But even here there is an inequality of values between the two.

4. This prejudice is completely unfounded. Cf. *The Nature of Sympathy.*

5. We find a particularly clear expression of this view in the sections on love of Thomas a Kempis' *Imitatio Christi.*

6. The later theological thesis according to which God has created the world "for his glorification" is foreign to the spirit of the Gospel. It is an element of ancient philosophy which has entered Christian theology. Only the thesis that God glorifies himself in his creation of love corresponds to the evangelical spirit.

7. Therefore the most profound contentment is not connected with the achievements of love (taken as an act of aspiration): it lies in love itself. "Thus God's joy in bestowing his gifts is greater than our joy in receiving them" (cf. François de Sales, *Treatise on the Love of God*, vol. I, ch 11).

Quite objectively, the ancients were fundamentally mistaken in defining love as an "aspiration" and a "need." Love may entail intense striving and yearning for the beloved, but in its essence it is an entirely different act. In the act of love, we rest contentedly in a value, regardless if this value has already been realized or if it is an object of aspiration. Cf. *The Nature of Sympathy.*

8. In his *Nichomachean Ethics,* Aristotle examines in detail how much love should "justly" be bestowed upon the various groups of men (such as parents, friends, children, strangers), depending on their degree of closeness to us. In the Christian perspective, this would be meaningful for benevolence and benefaction — but both are mere consequences of love. This approach is meaningless if applied to love as such, since the value of the human beings themselves is partly determined by the value of each act of love. Wherever the idea of justice transcends its purely rational factor (which demands that the same should be given to equals) — wherever it has somehow determined just *what* should be given to each — it presupposes love. In the rational sense, a man would be "just" even if he always equally harmed, hampered, or killed equals — and yet he would have no claim to the moral virtue designated as "justice."

9. Either him or a third person, "x," who knew him. [On the extension of the principle of solidarity, cf. *Formalismus,* section VI B.]

10. The basic question is whether the act of love is only a refinement, a shift or sublimation of original *sensory impulses* — instincts such as vital sympathy and, in the strongest form, the sexual urge — or whether it is an *originally spiritual* act. The latter assumption underlies the Christian idea of love. It implies that the act of love, with the laws that govern it, is *independent* of the physical and sensuous constitution. It merely combines with the urges and feelings of the affective sphere, in such a way that the affects come to determine the *selection* according to which (and the *intensity* with which) we factually apprehend the object of the intentionality of love. This is the conviction which underlies the Christian idea of love. Its objective justification has been discussed in detail in my book on sympathy, in the chapter "Love and Instinct." Here I only want to say this: if this view is correct, then the affective and vital sympathy (with its strict gradation according to similarity, etc.) cannot be considered as the *source* of love, but only as a *force that restricts and distributes* it — a force that makes it serve the vital goals. This does not make love a result and product of vital development.

11. As an example of a personality propelled by *ressentiment* we named the Church Father Tertullian. Already Nietzsche quotes a passage in which Tertullian declares heavenly bliss to be based on the sight of the torments of the damned. We may add his famous "Credo quia absurdum, credo quia ineptum" and his whole immoderate attitude toward ancient civilization and religion. All this shows that often he only *uses* the Christian values in order to satisfy his hatred of the ancient values. The development of a *ressentiment* Christian is excellently described in Conrad Ferdinand Meyer's short story "The Saint."

12. We purposely confine our exposition to this vital aspect, ignoring the fact that the purely spiritual acts and the laws that govern them — as well as their objects and the interrelations of these objects — cannot be understood by any philosophy based on "life." There are whole series of values and valuable acts which are *independent* of vital acts and values. The Christian's "security" is primarily a state of security in a world which is essentially *above* life and its vicissitudes. But this assertion cannot be our premise here, since Nietzsche — who formulated the thesis that *ressentiment* is the source of the Christian idea of love — rejects it and wants to subsume even the idea

of truth under the "vital values." It is sufficient to show that his view is mistaken even if we accept his own premise, according to which the maximum of life is the highest value. Concerning the true place of the "vital values" in the hierarchy of values, cf. my detailed discussion in *Formalismus,* part II. [Section V 5.]

13. Cf. my book *Der Tod und die Seele,* to be published shortly. [The author never published this book. In *Formalismus,* part II (1916), the projected study was several times announced under the title *Der Tod und das Fortleben.* After about 1916, the plan was extended, and the projected study was to bear the title *Vom Sinn des Todes.* A part of the notes was published in 1933 in the previously mentioned *Nachlassband,* under the title "Tod und Fortleben" (written about 1912/13).]

14. The characteristic of *"bliss"* in the Christian sense is that it rests securely and immutably in the core of the soul, in the midst of the variations and changes of those emotions. The experience of bliss contains the conviction that it cannot be destroyed from the outside. [On "bliss" as the deepest layer of feeling, and on the other layers of feeling, cf. *Formalismus,* section V 9.]

15. According to the *Fioretti* (ch. 10), Francis — when asked why he among all was chosen to guide men towards true life by his preaching replied as follows: "… His holy eyes saw none among the sinners who was more miserable than I, none more incompetent, none who was a greater sinner. In order to accomplish the miraculous work he planned, he found no creature on earth that was more miserable. Therefore he chose me, for he wished to shame the world with its nobility, with its pride, its strength, beauty, and wisdom …." In this we may be tempted to see *ressentiment.* However, when he refers to "nobility, pride, strength, beauty, wisdom of the world" and speaks about putting them to "shame," Francis only means that these values are subordinate to those of the kingdom of God. But the kingdom of God by no means derives its own value from its *contrast* to the "world": it bears its value in itself, *independently* of the "values of the world."

16. Therefore the emotion which Schopenhauer calls "pity" also springs from *ressentiment.* For Schopenhauer, its significance does not lie in the fact that it is an expression of love — quite on the contrary, he traces love to pity. Nor does he see in pity a factor leading to benevolence and benefaction. To him, pity is the supposed recognition that the will, which suffers from itself, is metaphysically identical in all individuals. All benevolence and benefaction based on it can only *detract* from this metaphysical knowledge, ensnaring us again in the world of individuation. Thus when his friends lament their miseries and misfortunes, Schopenhauer can only answer one thing over and over again: "See how true my philosophy is!" Cf. Schopenhauer's letters to Frauenstädt.

17. Cf. the conclusion of the verses of St. Theresa:

> "…
> For even if I hoped not as I hope,
> I still would love as I love."

(Cf. also Franz Brentano, Vom *Ursprung sittlicher Erkenntnis,* Leipzig, 1889, Notes). Or the passage in the prayer of St. Gertrude where she expresses the wish that Jesus

were as small and poor as she and that she were allpowerful and omniscient as God
— so that she could divest herself of what she had and come down to Jesus (cf. *Preces
Gertrudianae).* Or the wish of Meister Eckhart "that he would rather be in hell with
Jesus than in heaven without him." Such references could be multiplied at will. They
show how *completely unfounded* is the assertion of Immanuel Kant and many others
that all moral activity which has any reference to God is eudaemonistic and egoistic,
since it is guided by concern with reward and punishment. "Nothing is sweet that
does not lead me to God; may the Lord take away all he desires to give me, and give to
me *only himself*" (Augustinus, *Enarrationes* 2). Cf. the author's previously cited books,
*The Nature* of *Sympathy* and *Formalismus,* part II. [Cf. the criticism of eudaemonistic
ethics in *Formalismus,* section V, especially chapters 9 and 10.]

18. As we know, it is a matter of dispute whether the God of Aristotle even
knows about the world and its contents. The latest theory is Franz Brentano's [cf.
his work on Aristotle in the book *Grosse Denker,* edited by E. von Aster, vol. I,
1911, section VI, p. 166] who concludes that God, by knowing himself, at the same
time knows the world in himself. But this is based on the assumption that Aristotle
taught the evident superiority of inner observation — an affirmation which seems
questionable to me.

19. It goes without saying that by "attention" we do not mean self-analysis, but
the interest in (and care for) one's own salvation.

20. Cf. my typology of the delusions of sympathy in *The Nature of Sympathy,*
part I.

21. No one has shown this more clearly than Aristotle in his *Nichomachean
Ethics.* Cf. the chapter "Self-Love" in Book IX: by sacrificing his life and possessions
to his friend, man accomplishes the highest act of "self-love." For leaving the lower
goods to his friend, by his act of sacrifice he covers himself with the "glory of the
noble action, i.e., the higher good."

22. [On egoism, egotism, and self-love, cf. *Formalismus.* Cf. index of 4th ed.,
1954.]

23. This is not to justify the dictum in question, only to understand it.

24. Malebranche cites Paul's passage in support of his doctrine of the "sens in-
terne," which he sets up against his teacher Descartes, in whose opinion introspection
is evidently superior to external observation. Cf. *De la recherche de la vérité,* I.

25. Nietzsche ignores that Christian morality does *not* value poverty, chastity,
and obedience as such, but only the autonomous *act of freely renouncing* property,
marriage, and self-will, whose existence is presupposed and which are considered as
*positive goods.* Therefore J. H. Newman says that "genuine" asceticism is to admire
the earthly things by renouncing them. Cf. Nietzsche's treatise "What is the Meaning
of Ascetic Ideals?" It is entirely based on this misinterpretation.

26. Cf. the author's essay "Zur Rehabilitierung der Tugend" in *Vom Umsturz
der Werte,* notably the conclusion of the section on humility.

27. I have shown this in detail in *Formalismus.*

28. An example would be the respiration exercises etc. of Indian Yogis.

29. Cf. the essay "Die christliche Liebesidee und die gegenwärtige Welt" in *Vom
Ewigen im Menschen.*

30. Thus in the Pauline interpretation, Jesus himself dies on the cross out of love, spurred on by the urge of one who is secure in God to sacrifice himself for mankind.

31. In part II of *Formalismus,* the author has established this point in detail, refuting any "biological" ethics which makes all values relative to life. [Section V 5.] Cf. also the author's article "Ethik" in the *Jahrbuch für Philosophie,* Jahrgang II, ed. by Max Frischeisen-Köhler, Berlin 1914.

32. Cf. also Ernst Troeltsch's pertinent discussions in his works *Politische Ethik und Christentum* (Göttingen, 1904) and *Die Soziallehren der christlichen Kirchen und Gruppen,* vol. I (Tübingen, 1912; in English: *The Social Teaching of the Christian Churches,* tr. by Olive Wyon, New York, 1931).

33. In my book *Der Genius des Krieges und der deutsche Krieg* (Leipzig, 1915), I exhaustively proved that martial and Christian morality can form a unity of style.

34. Richard Rothe says perceptively and strikingly: "Christians fight — as if they did not fight."

35. "Forgiving" is a *positive* act which consists in freely sacrificing the positive value of expiation. Thus it presupposes the impulse of revenge instead of being based on its absence. In the same way, "toleration" (of an insult, for example) is not, as Nietzsche thinks, mere passive acceptance: it is a peculiar *positive* attitude of the person toward an impulse which does not want to be obstructed, a positive curbing of this impulse. This is why Christian morality opposes anaesthesia or the autosuggestive modification of pain by means of a judgment — such as the Stoic doctrine that "pain is no evil." Christian morality only indicates a new way to guide pain "correctly." Cf. my essay "Vom Sinn des Leides" in *Krieg und Aufbau* (Leipzig, 1916). [This essay was republished by the author, in a considerably extended form, in *Moralia* (1923), vol. I of the *Schriften zur Soziologie und Weltanschauungslehre.*]

36. Herbert Spencer, for example, construes the whole historical development of moral life in accordance with this principle. On the fallacy of the genetic view that the feeling of love and sympathy are mere epiphenomena of a growing solidarity of interests, cf. *The Nature of Sympathy,* part II, ch. VI.

37. The state of "social equilibrium."

# IV

## Ressentiment *and Modern Humanitarian Love*

1. In lecture 10 of his *Anweisung zum seligen Leben* (Berlin, 1806; Engl. translation *The Way towards the Blessed Life* by William Smith, London, 1849) Johann Gottlieb Fichte makes an extremely sharp distinction between the two ideas: "Finding that they live in God, he will love their existence. He deeply hates their existence without God, and precisely this is his love of their true being: that he hates their restrictive being." Cf. also what precedes this passage! Fichte shows "universal love of

mankind" to be identical with what should be called "hatred of mankind" according to his idea of love.

2. The traditional theories of "humanitarian love" also trace love of nature, of plants and animals, to the projection of human experiences into the forms of nature. On these fallacies cf. my book *The Nature of Sympathy*, part II, ch. I (2). While in the Christian view love of mankind as a species is grounded in *love of the world*, modern love of mankind has always been coupled with a particular *hatred of the world*, so that the "world" and "nature" have merely appeared as things to be dominated for human purposes.

3. On the source of the entirely fallacious view that love of the wider circle is *intrinsically* better than love of the smaller one, cf. my book on *The Nature of Sympathy*, notably part II, ch. VI (2: "The facts concerning the 'perspective of interests.'").

4. Part I of *The Nature of Sympathy* contains an exhaustive clarification of this confused question. It shows how the term "sympathy" is applied to several completely different phenomena which are often mistaken for each other. The book also contains a critique of the current theories concerning the origin of sympathy.

5. Jean-Jacques Rousseau as well explicitly derives love from pity. Therefore Schopenhauer cites him in support of his own theory.

6. In part I of Gustav Störring's *Moralpolitische Streitfragen* (Leipzig, 1903) we find an exact account of the historical development of the English theories on sympathy.

7. Cf. Charles Darwin, *The Descent of Man,* ch. V. [In the 1912 version of this essay, there is the following footnote at this point: "A precise analysis and critique of all these insufficient theories cannot be given here. I refer to the first volume of my ethics, which will appear shortly — also for a positive analysis of *sympathy.*" This shows that the study on sympathy was originally to be published in the framework of *Formalismus.* — On the critique of the English ethics of sympathy, cf. part I, ch. I of *The Nature of Sympathy.*]

8. On Darwin's and Spencer's mistakes, cf. *The Nature of Sympathy*, part I, ch. VIII, and part II, ch. V, VI.

9. Even before Nietzsche, Kant excellently developed this view in his anthropology, as Hans Vaihinger and Alois Riehl point out in their Nietzsche books. Already Mandeville's "Fable of the Bees" is a very justified satire on these English theories of sympathy.

10. Wilhelm Dilthey's judgment is correct. With reference to Bernard de Clairvaux and Francis of Assisi he writes: "Seen from the outside, it may appear contradictory that religious contemplation here goes together with active love in the service of one's brothers. ... This apparent contradiction ... springs from the fact that in Christianity, the surrender to the invisible continuity makes the soul sovereign and completely independent of the world and men, but at the same time places the soul in entirely new relations with other men" (*Das natürliche System der Geisteswissenschaften im 17. Jahrhundert, Gesammelte Schriften II*. Leipzig & Berlin, 1914, pp. 208-09).

11. In the sense that the principle of love neither supports nor condemns them.

12. Every feeling of pain or suffering caused by mere emotional contagion (such as, for example, the direct reproduction of a feeling of pain through the sight of an expression of pain) is accompanied by the urge *to remove its causes*. This urge differs in no way from the same tendency when the pain is *our* own — i.e., the action remains entirely "egoistic." Genuine "pity" has nothing whatever to do with such "contagion"! Then we are not "implicated" in another person's suffering: we remain detached from it. When old women infect each other by their crying, we truly cannot say that they "pity" each other. Cf. *The Nature of Sympathy*, part I, ch. II (3).

13. The state of mind of the typical Christian sicknurse is one 13. The state of mind of the typical Christian sicknurse is one firmness, serenity, vigor, and happiness in doing good, also "good nerves," and by no means that sentimental participation in the patient's state. This kind of "pity" serves to strengthen the gesture which asks for pity, so that he who pities and he who is pitied *mutually increase* their false suffering. Cf. my essay "Die psychologie der sogenannten Rentenhysterie und der rechte Kampf gegen das Übel" in *Vom Umsturz der Werte*.

14. [Cf. Goethe's *Travels in Italy*, Naples, 27 May 1787, with reference to Herder's *Outlines of a Philosophy of the History of Man*: "I am looking forward to Herder's Third Part .... I am certain that he excellently worked out mankind's beautiful dream of being better off one day. Moreover, as I myself must say, I think it is true that humanism will triumph at last; only I fear ...."]

15. [Cf. the introductory paragraph of "Probleme der Religion" in *Vom Ewigen im Menschen. Gesammelte Werke*, vol. 5 (Bern, 1954).]

16. This idea finds masterly artistic illustration in the valuations and world view of Ivan in Dostoevsky's *Brothers Karamazof*.

17. Sometimes the Church and religion themselves base the meaning and value of the love of God on the empirically existing positive goods and meaningful institutions, instead of basing all love of the world on the fact that it is "God's world." Then indeed the idea of the love of God has been falsified at the source, and the new ideal of the "love of man" is right in accusing it.

18. The best example I know is the history of the excellent prince Kropotkin, especially the story of his youth (cf. his autobiography). The early inner conflict with his father, who remarried after his beloved mother's death, gradually perverted the prince's essentially noble and gentle nature. He increasingly chose sides in favor of the servants of the home, came to negate on principle all positive values and ideals of the Russian state and people, and ended up by embracing anarchist ideas.

19. On the whole, the teaching of the later Stoics (especially Epictetus and Marcus Aurelius) is strongly determined by *ressentiment*. It would be an interesting task to show this in detail.

20. [This is the point to refer to the author's later statement, to the effect that on several occasions in *Ressentiment* he went too far in his judgment on universal humanitarian love. Cf. *The Nature of Sympathy*, part I, ch. VI, where the author indicates which of his assertions in *Ressentiment* he wants to discard and which he wants to maintain. Cf.also the preface of the 3rd ed. of *Vom Umsturz der Werte*.]

21. [From Friedrich Rückert's poem "Welt und Ich."]

22. Though M.P. Artsybashev's novel *Sanine,* which had such success and impact in Russia [it caused the movement of "Saninism" after its appearance in 1907] is very unpleasant and in many ways repulsive, it finds its justification in its opposition to this morbid, hysterical urge for political sacrifice which has grasped large sections of Russian youth. It is only sad that the novel finds nothing higher than erotic tasks to be put in the place of the political goals.

23. The same may be said of those repulsive religious pedagogues who dare — and quite honestly! — to recommend religious faith for the "others," merely to cement popular tradition and the means of education, while they themselves are far from sharing it. "Je suis athée — mais je suis catholique," Maurice Barrès is supposed to have said in the French Chamber once.

24. Cf. Ernst Troeltsch, *The Social Teaching* of *the Christian Churches.*

25. It was the theory and practice of the Jesuit order which gave decisive impetus to this process. In contrast with the principles of "self-sanctification" which ruled the other orders, especially that of the Benedictines, the Jesuits gave primacy to the "love of man." Here again, Jesuitism proves to be a descendant of modern *humanism* in the framework of the Christian Church. The compromises of the Jesuit moralists with human *frailty,* criticized in Pascal's *Lettres provinciales,* indicate a steady advance of the "modern love of man" as against the Christian idea of love.

26. Augustine rejects every moral motivation based "on hope for reward and fear of punishment." Later it is admitted for pedagogical reasons. Thomas of Aquinas distinguishes between "childlike" and "slavish fear." He, too, rejects the latter.

27. In Plato's view, we owe the innate ideas to a supersensory experience which *varies* in richness and intensity in the different classes and types of profession. In this respect Plato's doctrine of "innate ideas" differs entirely from the modern theory of the same name, which has been developing since Descartes.

28. This notion, as well as the recognition of an independent and justified "rational" sphere which exists below the sphere of grace (in religion, law, morality, etc.) does not entirely prevail until Thomas of Aquinas. In his perspective, the Pauline-Augustinian religion of love and grace and the religion based on rules and laws are two "purposive stages" *(Zweckstufen* — Ernst Troeltsch). These new versions represent the first incursion of the young bourgeois ideals into the ideological system of the Christian Church. Cf. Werner Sombart's numerous pertinent passages in *Der Bourgeois* (Munich & Leipzig, 1913), especially pp. 303 and 307. (pp. 236 and 238-39 in the English translation, *The Quintessence of Capitalism,* translated by M. Epstein, New York, 1915). Cf. also my essay "Der Bourgeois und die religiösen Mächte" in *Vom Umsturz der Werte.* Cf. further Johann Adam Möhler's interesting remarks in *Die Einheit in der Kirche* (Tübingen, 1825), which prove that the Church Fathers knew no strict separation between natural theology and revealed positive theology. [On natural religion and theology and revealed, positive religion and theology, cf. the author's essay "Probleme der Religion" in *Vom Ewigen im Menschen.*]

29. Cf. Carl Prantl, *Geschichte der Logik im Abendlande* (Leipzig, 1855-1870), vol. I. Cf. further the excellent Introduction to Johann Adam Möhler *Patrologie.*

30. What Luther rejects as useless for salvation is not only the external act which is morally relevant — to say nothing of the mere observance of Church ceremonial. His concept of "works" also includes *the inner act of love.*

31. Sombart, in his previously mentioned book, seems to overlook this fact — which applies even more to Calvinism, in a different form — and its weighty consequences. Contrary to Max Weber, he argues that Thomism had more influence on the development of the "capitalist spirit" than original Protestantism. Cf. my essay "Der Bourgeois und die religiösen Mächte" in *Vom Umsturz der Werte.*

32. In a sense which contradicts the postulate "Love thy neighbor as thyself."

33. Cf. Johann Adam Möhler pertinent discussion in his *Symbolik* (1832; new ed. Regensburg, 1914) — especially §25, "Höchster Punkt der Unter-suchung." (English translation: *Symbolism,* tr. James Burton Robertson, London, 1843 and New York, 1844, § 25: "The Culminating Point of Inquiry").

34. [On love of self, of one's neighbor, and of God, cf. *Formalismus.*]

35. Love, according to Kant, is a "pathological sensory affect" which can claim no place among the genuine motives of moral action. Moreover, one cannot "control" it. This judgment, of course, is influenced by the theory and practice of the modern love of mankind. For the Christian authors, love is neither an "affect" nor a "state of feeling," but a goal-directed spiritual act. Cf. part II of *Formalismus,* where I demonstrate that Kant seriously misinterprets the postulate "Love God above all and love thy neighbor as thyself," making it agree artificially with his ethics. [Cf. especially section IV 2 (4th ed., 1954, p. 234 ff).]

36. The so-called "ethical" branch of political economy, and especially the "Christian ethical" one, is itself nothing but a product of this turbid mixture. It merely shows that its partisans know virtually nothing about "genuine ethics." The recent demand for an entirely "value-free" economic science is fully justified.

37. It is a basic element in Ignatius' "exercises" that he transfers the relation of military discipline which exists between a general and his army to the relation between the "self" and the "thoughts."

38. On the essential difference between *"Leib"* and *"Körper,"* part II of *Formalismus.* [Cf. section VI A, 3f.]

* In Scheler's distinction, the *"Körper"* is the body apprehended by external perception, as an object like all others. In contrast to this "body as-an-object," the *"Leib" is* the "body-of-the-subject" — i.e., the subject apprehends it by inner perception, independently of all sensory capacity.

39. On the difference between positive and negative asceticism, cf. also my essays "Über östliches und westliches Christentum" and "Vom Sinn des Leides" in my book *Krieg und Aufbau.* [About the essay "Vom Sinn des Leides," cf. footnote 35 of ch. III.] Cf. further Ernst Troeltsch, *The Social Teaching of the Christian Churches.*

V

## Ressentiment *and Other Value Shifts in Modern Morality*

1. It was neither the purpose of this essay to establish the genealogy of modern "bourgeois" morality as a whole, nor to gain purely historical insight into the ultimate motive forces which led to its formation. Yet I am very pleased that that section of Werner Sombart's book *Der Bourgeois* which treats this subject (cf. also my essay "Der Bourgeois" in *Vom Umsturz der Werte)* corroborates and strengthens my assertions and analyses more than I had dared to hope. Starting from the present essay, Sombart goes so far as to say that *"ressentiment* is the basic trait" in the family records of the Florentine weaver Leon Battista Alberti, in whom he sees the first pronounced and typical expression of the bourgeois spirit and morality-long before Benjamin Franklin, Daniel Defoe, et al. I shall quote the whole passage. Referring to *ressentiment,* Sombart writes:

"I believe that it also played a role in the history of the capitalist spirit. I see it in this elevation of petty bourgeois principles, which were born from necessity, to universal and valuable maxims of life — i.e., in the doctrine according to which the 'bourgeois' virtues are great human virtues in an absolute sense. Those who branded the doings of the great lords as wicked were men of middle-class status (and often, no doubt, *déclassé* noblemen) who looked on these doings with jealousy. They preached the renunciation of a seigneurial way of life which deep down they really loved and desired, but from which they were excluded by external circumstances or subjective reasons. *Ressentiment is the basic trait in Alberti's family records.* I have already cited several passages which reflect a downright comical and childish hatred against the 'signori' from whose circle he was excluded. These could easily be multiplied. And his tirades against seigneurial conduct, the seigneurial pleasures of the hunt, the customs of the clientele system, etc., always end in pharisaic praise of his own worthy middle-class simplicity. It is true that everything contributed to strengthen Alberti's middle-class view of life: his commercial interests, his philosophical readings, his confessor's exhortations. But the immoderate abuse in which he indulges whenever he refers to the 'signori' — and which indicates that his experiences with them must have been very bad — show that *ressentiment* is perhaps the strongest of the motives which led him to his solid middle-class world view.

Throughout all eras, *ressentiment* remained the firmest pillar of bourgeois morality. The statement that 'the grapes are sour' is still proclaimed by the virtuous 'bourgeois,' who likes to console himself in this way.

But wherever and whenever the guilds, in which 'bourgeois' convictions ruled by sheer necessity — but which liked 'to make a virtue out of necessity' — gain prestige and influence, so that at last they 'set the fashion,' their mentality inevitably becomes an acknowledged and laudable one. Their spirit becomes the general spirit. This process took place with particular clarity in Florence, which was therefore entirely impregnated with the bourgeois spirit as early as the 15th century, while other cities (such as Venice) still preserved their seigneurial character for a long time" (from Werner Sombart, *Der Bourgeois,* pp. 439-40. In the English translation, *The Quintessence* of *Capitalism,* pp. 340-41).

I also point to Sombart's own excellent characterizations of modern bourgeois morality (cf. especially the second and third section of book II). They completely confirm my thesis that the Christian ideas of virtue and morality are gradually falsified, are imperceptibly transformed into an exaltation of those human qualities and units of action which make bourgeois business prosper — all this while the old venerable names and Christian pathos are maintained! What Frank Wedekind says about "sin" in general can often literally apply to modern *sham* valuations: it is "a mythological designation for bad business"!

2. [On "hereditary good" and "hereditary guilt," cf. *Formalismus,* section VI B 3 (on the autonomy of the person).]

3. Marcus Porcius Cato was an ancient bourgeois (in Sombart's sense) and a man of *ressentiment* in more than one respect. Friedrich Leo writes that Cato's moralism sprang from his feeling of being excluded horn the old Roman nobility. Cf. especially Cato's work on agriculture. (Friedrich Leo, *Geschichte der römischen Literatur,* I, Berlin, 1913).

4. We are far from agreeing with Johann Friedrich Herbart's view, according to which moral blame and praise apply with "equal vigor" to strictly determined acts of volition, so that there is no essential difference between moral and aesthetic values. We too believe that moral value is exclusively attached to the "free" act. But this does not mean that an intrinsically "free" act (i.e., an act which is not determined by the laws of motivation, though it does follow the laws of what is right) is subject to moral value or disvalue only if it is caused by the same individual by whom it is carried out. The cause of a "free act" may also lie outside of the individual, in tradition or heredity. Cf *Formalismus,* part II [Cf. footnote 2 of ch. V.]

5. Cf. my book *Der Genius des Krieges und der deutsche Krieg.*

6. In an analogous way, the economic forms of organization and labor can change only within the framework set by political power relations. Thus the transformation of the latter follows a causality of its own, which cannot be understood in "economic" terms. [This note was added to the 1919 edition. At that time, the author worked on the philosophy of history. Those studies have not been published. On the doctrine of the independent variable within historical "real factors" *(historische Realfaktoren),* cf. the later study "Probleme einer Philosophie des Wissens" (1924), part I, in *Die Wissensformen und die Gesellschaft* (1926). Vol. 8 of *Gesammelte Werke.*]

7. Herbart carried this idea to the extreme with his concept of a mind without native dispositions.

8. In part II of *Formalismus* [section VI B 4, ad 4] I established the principle of moral solidarity in detail. On its application, cf. my book *Vom Ewigen im Menschen,* especially "Die christliche Liebesidee und die gegenwärtige Welt."

9. For as we saw, it is the essence of the modern love of mankind that the "sensory system" is not considered as a limitation of "love," but as its root, and that the good deed is not valued as a sign of the act of love, but that the act of love itself is valued

merely as the cause of an externally palpable and practicable benefaction. According to Thomas à Kempis, "God looks only at the giver's love, not at the lover's gift." This valuation is reversed by modern humanitarian love.

10. The inability to "accept presents" is a particularly philistine trait of modern morality. Cf. my remarks on humility in the essay "Zur Rehabilitierung der Tugend" (in *Vom Umsturz der Werte)*.

11. I hope that the idea of moral solidarity will not be equated with the modern valuation according to which a "solidarity of interests" (for example, as it exists among workers on strike, or between the members of a trust and the outsider) creates a moral obligation of "participation."

12. The genuine Christian idea of solidarity in guilt and merit is wonderfully expressed in the words and actions of the old staretz, in Dostoevsky's *Brothers Karamazof.*

13. [Cf. the next section.]

14. On the enormous role which this basic distrust between men plays in Calvinism, cf. Max Weber's profound studies on Calvinism and the spirit of capitalism.

15. It needs no special mention that both general and criminal psychology have now completely broken with the doctrine of equal moral dispositions. Yet nearly all the institutions of learning and law which sprang from the movement of liberalism are still based on this supposition, though science has discarded it long ago. Cf. the interesting material in Carl Rath, *Über die Vererbung* yon *Dispositionen zum Verbrechen* (Stuttgart, 1914).

16. The idea of "justice" as such demands no equality — it only demands equivalent conduct when the circumstances have *equal* value. Walther Rathenau writes in his *Reflexionen* (Leipzig, 1908): "The idea of justice is based on envy." This applies only to the *falsification* of the idea of "justice," which is based on *ressentiment,* and *not* to its genuine core.

17. Here I cannot prove the fact that "values" are ultimate independent phenomena and neither mere "feelings" or "dispositions" (though they reach us in the *function* of feeling, just as color reaches us in the function of seeing), nor mere "abstractions" based on acts of judgment. Part II of *Formalismus* contains a detailed analysis of these questions, including a critique of all ruling theories of value. [Section IV.] Cf. in addition my article "Ethik" in *Philosophische Jahrbücher,* II. Jahrgang, 1914, ed. by Max Frischeisen-Köhler.

18. Cf. ch. I of the present essay, where I describe how the true values shine through the "false values."

19. We do recognize the difference between Kant's theory and the theory of "generic consciousness." But the genuine objectivity of values is also denied if it is determined as the X of a possible "generally valid" volition. For although the "good" is generally valid, it can by no means be defined as the maxim which is suitable for a generally valid principle. [*Formalismus* contains a critique of the subjectivist conception of being and value, of the identification of objectivity and general validity. Cf. Index.]

20. Therefore the very title of Nietzsche's work *Human, All-Too-Human* is a step in the right direction!

21. The immediate "self-evidence" of a form of being and an object philosophically *precedes* any quest for the generally valid "criterion" for affirming its existence. Cf. my essay "Versuche einer Philosophie des Lebens" in *Vom Umsturz der Werte.*

22. We use the term "world view" in the sense of Wilhelm von Humboldt, designating the *structure* according to which a race, a people, or a period *apprehends* the world. Those who share a certain "world view" may be unaware of it. It is sufficient that given reality is structured and accented in accordance with this world view. Even the "science" of a period is always conditioned by its "world view" *(Weltanschauung).* Cf. especially Wilhelm von Humboldt, "Über das vergleichende Sprachstudium" [first appeared in the "Historisch-Philologischen Abhandlungen der Berliner Akademie, 1820-21.] Cf. my treatise "Vom Wesen der Philosophie" in *Vom Ewigen im Menschen.*

23. In my book *Der Genius des Krieges und der deutsche Krieg,* I show in detail how the reversal of this rank order between "nobility" and "usefulness" has especially subordinated the values of martial morality to those of mercantile morality, most fundamentally in England.

24. I here abstain from citing the full and often described abundance of facts which show a disproportion between the advancement of life and the sensuous urge for pleasure — the whole theme of sweet poison and bitter medicine.

25. If we reduced the criminal laws of present-day Europe to the rank order of the legal *values* which is implied in them, we would see that the vital values are everywhere subordinated to the values of utility. Injury to the latter is punished more severely than harm done to the former. An example is the relation between bodily injury and theft. During the World War, this perversion of values became downright grotesque. The European states made far greater demands on the life and blood of their citizens than on their property. How prudent and hesitating were all encroachments on the system of property!

26. On the objective hierarchy, and on the corresponding rank order of the values themselves, cf. *Formalismus,* part I and II, especially section II 5. For the concrete application of this law, cf. my book *Die Ursachen des Deutschenhasses,* 2nd. ed. (Leipzig, 1919).

27. The specifically modern urge to work (the unbridled urge for acquisition, unlimited by need, is nothing but its consequence) is by no means due to a way of thinking and feeling which *affirms* life and the world, as it existed for example during the Italian Renaissance. It grew primarily on the soil of somber Calvinism, which is hostile to pleasure. Calvinism sets a transcendent and therefore unattainable goal for work ("workers in the honor of God"). At the same time, work here serves as a narcotic for the believers, enabling them to support the doubt and uncertainty whether they are "called" or "elect." Max Weber and Ernst Troeltsch have shown this very well in their studies on the Calvinist origin of modern capitalism. Cf. my two essays on the bourgeois in *Vom Umsturz der Werte* and my book *Die Ursachen des Deutschenhasses.*

In Sombart's opinion, the "Jewish spirit" is one of the chief causes of the development of the capitalist social structure. It is quite in agreement with my thesis that this spirit, which has had a lien on *ressentiment* for a long time, plays a major role in this process.

28. In his book *Mehr Freude,* bishop Paul Wilhelm von Keppler has very subtly illustrated this contradiction. To the question "How do I attain more joy?" he gives the seemingly tautological, but in fact very profound answer: "Rejoice." This implies that the function of rejoicing, of enjoyment, etc., is entirely independent of the sensory quantities of pleasure and displeasure, and of the stimuli which correspond to them. Therefore it can be subjected to a cultivation and education *of its own,* which is not furthered, but turned into its opposite by the search for and the production of new stimulants.

29. One of the most essential among the partial processes which bring about the concrete subordination of the values of pleasure to those of utility is the gradual transition of the big cities from "cities of consumption" — the character of all older big cities, according to Sombart in *Luxus und Kapitalismus* — to "cities of production."

30. The development of the capitalist "economic mentality" — the transformation of an acquisitive urge which is guided by the desire to live according to one's status into an acquisitive urge which reserves for "subsistence" only those goods that are *left* when the *automatic* tendency of the "business" to grow has been satisfied — is only a *partial process* of the general transformation of the leading ethos. Compare the above with my essay "Der Bourgeois" in *Vom Umsturz der Werte.*

31. Cf. my book *Der Genius des Krieges und der deutsche Krieg.*

32. In an analogous way, the idea of justice which governs modern international law wants justice in arbitration to be independent of the value of the states involved.

33. Cf. Werner Sombart, *Der Bourgeois,* p. 139 (in English translation, *The Quintessence of Capitalism*: p. 106).

34. But I must say that our "youth" is in process of rediscovering this idea. In this I see one of the surest signs that the modern bourgeois spirit is being gradually overcome.

35. Cf. preceding note.

36. Cf. Herbert Spencer Jennings, *Contributions to the Study of the Behavior of Lower Organisms* (Washington, 1904).

37. Cf. Oskar Kohnstamm, "Zwecktätigkeit und Ausdruckstätigkeit," *Arch. Z. der ges. Psychologie,* vol. XXIX, 1913.

38. On the fundamental error of this view, cf. my previously cited book on *Formalismus,* part I and II. Cf. also my theory of volition in part I. [Cf. the critique of utilitarianism in the doctrine of life in section V 5; furthermore, the theory of volition in section III.]

39. Cf. my book *Der Genius des Krieges und der deutsche Krieg,* section I.

40. In his book *L'évolution créatrice,* Henri Bergson has said many penetrating things about these questions. But we think it can be shown that he commits one error: he fails to distinguish between the principles of pure logic and the principles of the logic which is used in mechanistic physics. Thus he is led to the impossible attempt of deriving even the principles of "pure" logic from vital tendencies. However,

the principles of pure logic are far from leading to the principles of mechanics and the mechanical principle of causality. Cf. *Formalismus,* part II, last section. [Section VI A, 3 g.]

41. My book *Phänomenologie und Erkenntnistheorie,* which will appear shortly, contains more detailed arguments in favor of this view. [The author never published this book. The manuscript was published posthumously in the previously mentioned *Nachlassband* (1933). It does not contain the discussion of mechanist and pragmatist theory which the author still wanted to include.]

42. This word is not meant to designate the political democracy of any particular period, which may very well represent an aristocratic scale of values. Cf. my essay "Die Zukunft des Kapitalismus" in *Vom Umsturz der Werte.* Cf. also "Bemerkungen zum Geiste und den ideellen Grundlagen der Demokratien der grossen Nationen" in my book *Krieg und Aufbau.* [The author republished the latter essay in 1924, in the volume *Nation* of the *Schriften zur Soziologie und Weltanschauungslehre.*]

43. The principle of solidarity has a parallel in biology. It is the view that *any* part of a fecundated cell can in principle grow into *any* organ and can stand for everything, provided that it has not already been assigned a special task through previous organ formation. On the ethical principle of solidarity, cf. *Formalismus,* part II [section VI B 4, ad 4] and *The Nature of Sympathy.*

44. I use these terms like Ferdinand Tönnies in *Gemeinschaft und Gesellschaft* (2nd ed., 1912. In English: *Fundamental Concepts of Sociology.* Translated and supplemented by Charles P. Loomis. New York, Cincinnati, etc., 1940). In *The Nature of Sympathy* I attempted to offer a new definition of the essential types of human association ("community," "society," "mass") on the basis of the respective phenomenal ways in which the "other mind" presents itself. Cf. also *Formalismus,* part II.

45. The historical documentation of this affirmation can be found in Sombart's *Der Bourgeois (The Quintessence of Capitalism).* Sombart cites an astounding amount of evidence which shows that everywhere the basic attitudes of pirates, adventurers, schemers, Jews, colonists, foreigners, heretics, et al., increasingly determine the mentality of *normal* economic life.

46. Spencer is thus necessarily led to pacifism, as I show in my book Der *Genius des Krieges und der deutsche Krieg.*

47. This point has been excellently clarified by Jakob von Uexküll in his recent book *Bausteine zu einer biologischen Weltanschauung* (Munich, 1913).

48. *The last two sentences are extremely obscure in the original. The translation adopted appears to come closest to what the author appears to have had in mind.

49. Oskar Hertwig has recently formulated an equivalent principle in his *Beiträge zur Vererbungslehre.* Cf. also the proofs for the mechanical character of vital processes which Hans Driesch gives in his *Science and Philosophy of the Organism* (London, 1908). However, we cannot agree with Driesch's positive system.

50. [Cf. *Formalismus,* section III.]

51. Cf. Henri Bergson, *L'évolution créatrice.* The relation between the organism and the surroundings has recently been characterized more correctly by Jakob von Uexküll in his book *Umwelt und Innenwelt der Tiere* (Berlin, 1909). Cf. also his theory about *Merkwelten* in *Bausteine zu einer biologischen Weltanschauung.* On organ

and tool, cf. also Conway Lloyd Morgan in his book *Habit and Instinct* (London & New York, 1896).

52. We consider the cultural value to be "higher" than the vital value. However, this whole domain of values will be ignored here. Cf. *Formalismus,* part I and II. [Cf. especially section II B 5 and section V 5.]

53. Of course we do not want to question the value of the mechanical view of nature *as such.* We only impugn its false epistemological *dignity,* if it is either conceived metaphysically or traced to the *a priori* of a "pure" intellect. On the true meaning of this view of nature, cf. my book *Phänomenologie und Erkenntnistheorie,* which will appear shortly. [Cf. footnote 41 of ch. V.]

54. Is it by chance that the greatest achievement of *ressentiment* in the modern era, the French Revolution, coincides with the most extreme domination of the mechanical world view? In my book *Die Ursachen des Deutschenhasses* I demonstrated, continuing along the lines of the present essay, that *ressentiment* also played a role in the genesis of Germanophobia.

55. [Cf. the essay "Zum Sinn der Frauenbewegung" in *Vom Umsturz der Werte.*]

# INDEX

Adam, 81, 99, 130, 139-140
Aeschylus, 36
Alberti, 113, 141
altruism, 62, 64, 86-88
Ananias, 76
anthropomorphism, 116
anxiety, 42-43, 48, 60-61, 131
Aquinas, Thomas, 95, 139
Aristotle, 15-16, 56, 89, 133, 135
Artsybashev, 139
asceticism, 70-71, 89, 94-95, 105, 108-110, 114, 135, 140
Augustine, St., 56, 59, 90, 139
Aurelius, Marcus, 138

Bacon, Francis, 115
Bain, Alexander, 81
Barrès, Maurice, 139
Benedictines, 139
Bentham, Jeremy, 80, 120
Bergson, Henri, 122, 145-146
Bismarck, O. von, 39
bliss, 23, 59-60, 62, 88, 133-134
Bossuet, Jacques, 83
bourgeoisie, 40, 46, 91, 110
Brentano, Franz, 134-135

Calvinism, 140, 143-144
capitalism, 75, 108, 129, 142-146
Cato, Marcus Porcius, 142
Christianity, 41, 65, 73, 75, 87, 90-91, 93-94, 98, 101, 137
civilization, 2, 30, 36, 38, 45, 51-52, 94, 104-105, 108-109, 113-116, 122-123, 125, 128, 133
Clairvaux, 137
class hatred, 43, 48, 93
cognition, 35, 105-106
communism, 75-76
community, 38, 69, 72, 74, 76-77, 79-80, 83, 86-87, 92, 113, 118-120
Comte, Auguste, 51, 85-87, 93
consciousness, 25, 33-35, 43-45, 49, 55, 65, 117, 120, 129, 143
Copernican system, 52

covenant, 62-63
culture, 2, 5, 108, 115

Darwin, Charles, 82, 130, 137
Defoe, Daniel, 141
deity, 56-58, 63
democratism, 118
Descartes, René, 2, 44, 95, 100, 114, 120, 135, 139
Dilthey, Wilhelm, 137
Dostoevsky, Feodor, 130, 138, 143
Driesch, Hans, 146

Eckhart, Meister, 135
ego, 14, 21, 39, 94-95, 118
egoism, 60, 64, 135
Ellis, Havelock, 130
Enlightenment, 104
entropy, 121
envy, 17, 25-26, 29-30, 38-39, 42-44, 46, 65, 85, 99, 103, 109, 129, 143
Epictetus, 138
Epicureans, 60
equality, 28-29, 34, 55, 84, 89, 91, 100-102, 143
Essenianism, 94
ethics, 5, 9, 12, 15-16, 45, 51-53, 131-133, 135-137, 140
Eumenides, 36
existence, 1-3, 28-31, 34, 43, 47-48, 59-60, 62, 68, 72, 74-75, 88-89, 99, 102-106, 113, 118, 131, 135-136, 144

fear, 27, 42-43, 46, 48, 60, 69, 84, 101, 131, 139
Fichte, J.G., 84, 136
Francis of Assisi, 61, 134, 137
Franklin, Benjamin, 141
French Revolution, 53, 84, 93, 110, 128, 147

God, 4, 24, 33-34, 40, 55, 57-58, 60, 62-63, 65-67, 71-75, 79-83, 85, 87, 89-92, 95, 98, 101, 112, 132, 134-136, 138, 140

Goethe, Johann Wolfgand von, 30, 47-48, 84, 131, 138
Gogol, Nicolai, 130
Guyau, J.M., 45, 73, 128, 131

Hegel, G.W.F., 41
Hellas, 42
Hellenistic philosophy, 95
Herbart, J.F., 142
Herder, 84, 138
Hertwig, Oskas, 146
hierarchy, 35, 45, 52, 66, 83, 103, 106, 108, 110, 113-114, 125, 132, 134, 144
Hölderlin,Friedrich, 42
humanitarian love, 79-95, 100, 136, 138, 143
Hume, David, 81
Hutcheson, Francis, 81

Ignatius of Loyola, 94, 140
impotence, 9, 24-26, 29-30, 32, 34, 36, 42, 45-47, 70
industrialism, 116, 124-125

James, William, 131, 140
Jennings, Herber Spencer, 145
Jesuits, 139
Jesus, 23, 44, 60-61, 66-69, 72-75, 91, 100, 134-136

Kant, Immanuel, 2, 14, 16, 84, 93, 97, 104, 121, 135, 137, 140, 143
Kempis, Thomas à, 132, 143
Keppler, Paul Wilhelm von, 145

labor, 29, 97, 99, 114, 117, 124, 142
Leo, Friedrich, 142
Locke, John, 99-100
love, 3-4, 6, 11, 13, 15-16, 20, 23-24, 30, 32, 37, 42, 44, 46, 55-65, 68, 70-74, 76-77, 79-95, 97, 100, 112, 118, 131-134, 136-140, 142-143
Luther, Martin, 68-69, 91-92, 140

majority, 9, 120
Malebranche, Nicholas de, 135

Mammon, 75
Mandeville, Bernard, 137
Marx, Karl, 33
Melanchthon, Philip, 91
Middle Ages, 38, 42, 83, 108, 114
Mill, John, Stuart, 16, 51
Milton, Johm, 129
Möhler, Johann Adam, 130, 139-40
Montanism, 130
morality, 24, 37, 40, 45, 48, 52-53, 55-77, 82, 88-89, 91-94, 97-125, 132, 135-136, 139, 141-144
Morgan, 147

Neo-Platonism, 94
Newman, J.H., Cardinal, 135
Nietzsche, Friedrich, 20, 23-24, 29, 40-42, 45, 48, 53, 55, 67, 70-75, 79, 83, 85, 88, 91, 93-94, 100, 127, 133, 135-137, 143

organ, 105, 116-118, 120-125, 128, 146

parliament, 129, 131
Pascal, Blaise, 4, 45, 76, 87, 139
Paul, 44, 59, 70, 131, 135, 145
perversion, 49, 97, 107, 110, 144
perversion of values, 144
phenomenology, 3-4, 13, 22-49, 127, 132
Plato, 15, 55-56, 72, 139
pleasure, 29, 72, 77, 88-89, 107-109, 120, 144-145
progress, 2, 34, 118, 125, 129
proletariat, 29, 40
property, 28, 32, 62, 73, 76, 93, 99, 102, 107, 114, 124, 128, 135, 144
Ptolemaic, 52

Ranke, Leopold von, 34, 129
Rath, Carl, 143
Rathenau, Walther, 143
regression
repression, 25, 28, 37, 43-44, 69
*Ressentiment*, 2-49, 51-53, 55-77, 79-95, 97-147

revenge, 6-7, 17, 23-28, 37, 39-45, 48-49, 56, 65, 67, 70, 75, 85, 99, 127-128, 136
Ribot, T.A., 35
Ricardo, David, 99
Riegl, 132
Riehl, Alois, 137
Rothe, Richard, 136
Rousseau, Jean-Jacques, 34, 81, 84, 137
Rückert, Friedrich, 138

St Augustine (see Augustine, St.)
St Francis, 61 (see also Francis of Assisi)
St Gertrude, 134
St Theresa, 134
Saint Victor, Hugo de, 63
Saninism, 139
Satan, 129
Schiller, Friedrich, 84
Schlegel, Friedrich, 42
Schopenhauer, Arthur, 134, 137
self-control, 112-113
self-hatred, 64-65, 87
Sigwart, 130
Simmel, Georg, 31
Smith, Adam, 81, 99, 136
social structure, 36, 110, 144
socialism, 75, 93
solidarity, 15, 68, 91, 100-101, 118, 133, 136, 142-143, 146
Sombart, Werner, 38, 113, 128-129, 139-142, 144-146
Sparta, 71
Spencer, Herbert, 51, 77, 82, 116, 121, 124-125, 136-137, 145-146
Spinoza, Baruch, 34, 41, 75
Steinmetz, S.R., 128
Stoics, 89, 138

Tertullian, 41, 130, 133
Tolstoi, Leo, 130
Tönnies, Ferdinand, 146
tool, 116, 120, 123-125, 147
totality, 19, 33, 80, 116, 121-122, 125
Troeltsch, Ernst, 136, 139-140, 144

Uexküll, Jakob von, 146
ultramontanism, 93

utilitarianism, 93, 145

Vaihinger, Hans, 137
value, 6-13, 15, 17, 23, 25, 27, 30-36, 38, 41, 45-49, 51-53, 55-56, 58, 60-65, 68, 70-77, 80, 82-85, 87-88, 97-125, 128-129, 131-136, 138, 141-143, 145, 147

Weber, Max, 140, 143-144
Wedekind, Frank, 142
William II, 93
Worringer, Wilhelm, 132